EVERY WOMAN'S
QUICK & EASY
CAR CARE

A Worry-Free Guide to Car Troubles, Trials & Travels

EVERY WOMAN'S
QUICK & EASY
CAR CARE

A Worry-Free Guide to Car Troubles, Trials & Travels

Bridget Kachur

STOREY
BOOKS

The mission of Storey Publishing is to serve our customers by publishing practical information that encourages personal independence in harmony with the environment.

Edited by Nancy W. Ringer
Art direction by Meredith Maker
Cover design by Guido Barrata
Text design by Wendy Palitz and Susan Bernier
Layout and production by Susan Bernier and Erin Lincourt
Black and white illustrations by Terry Dovaston
Indexed by Lynda Stannard, Thistle Index

Storey books are available for special premium and promotional uses and for customized editions. For further information, please call Storey's Custom Publishing Department at 1-800-793-9396.

Printed in the United States by R.R. Donnelley, Crawfordsville
10 9 8 7 6 5 4 3 2 1

Library of Congress Cataloging-in-Publication Data

Kachur, Bridget.
    Every woman's quick & easy car care : a worry-free guide to car troubles, trials & travels / Bridget Kachur.
        p.   cm.
Includes index.
    ISBN 1-58017-451-5 (alk. paper)
    1. Automobiles—Popular works. 2. Automobiles—Maintenance and repair—Popular works. I. Title.
    TL146.5 .K33 2002
    629.28'72—dc21
                                                    2002001117

To the two loves of my life — my daughter and my fuzzy son.

Acknowledgments

Dad, this guidebook could never have happened without you.

A special thanks also to Nancy and the rest of the folks at Storey Books.

I am so glad, Nancy, that you sent that first note of inquiry.

CONTENTS

INTRODUCTION

My automotive education started innocently enough. Dad loved to fix cars, and there was always an old, beat-up car or two sitting out in our driveway, waiting for repairs. As for me, hanging out in the kitchen with Mom didn't exactly rev up my engine. I liked to be out with Dad, handing him screwdrivers and wrenches, "helping" with the work, getting my hands dirty. I'd hang over the front of the engine with him, peering down into the mysterious depths, trying to see in the tangled strangeness of it the beautiful machine that Dad could see. It took awhile, but gradually I learned to use the tools and make sense of what I was looking at. Eventually I could change mufflers, radiator hoses, shock absorbers, water pumps, dirty engine oil, and whatever else an ailing automobile could throw at me, all on my own.

The enjoyment I found in those hands-on experiences led me toward an automotive career. I kept fixing cars, but now for other people. Teaching auto mechanics was a natural progression. For a brief period, I even sold cars. Today, although I still sometimes take a break to get under the hood, I focus on writing about cars. The written word can reach a great audience, and I think it's important for all women to see that they can become competent in handling their own vehicles.

And don't we live in an automobile-obsessed society! Even when I was a kid, Dad never had to worry about whether one of his fixed-up clunkers would sell. No sooner had he made the necessary repairs than a knock sounded on the back door. "Sold!" he'd say, congratulating the new car owner as they shook hands. It's not much different today. Who doesn't look on with envy as a lucky driver passes by in *our* dream car? Antique car shows are growing in popularity, and many folks take test drives at dealerships just for fun. Even young kids pass time on the stoop by trading tales of the slick, luxurious cars they'll drive when they grow up.

The incredible volume of different makes and models of cars available today shows how diverse a people we are when it comes driving. *Why* we choose a particular car opens a whole universe for discussion. Everyone knows that a car is a big financial investment — but it's more than that. It's an expression of ourselves and a statement about our lifestyle. When we have kids to cart around to baseball, hockey, and ballet, we often want a car that is both roomy and safe, such as an SUV or minivan. When we commute long distances to work, we want a car that is comfortable, dependable, and fuel-efficient. Our first set of wheels is often a used car, perhaps kept on the road only by the sheer willpower of a highly skilled mechanic. And sometimes we pick out a car just because we happen to like that particular color.

No matter what kind of car you have, how you deal with its mechanical needs is a matter of choice. Your choice. You can be a very responsible car owner even if you don't know what a lug nut looks like or what the heck it's used for. You may have concluded that the automotive shop looks after the maintenance and repairs very nicely, thank you. You pay the bills, you're satisfied with the service, and you certainly don't want to know how to open the hood, never mind find the oil dipstick. That is absolutely okay. You'll use this book simply to gain a basic understanding of how a car works and, more important, to learn what to do in an emergency.

If you're interested in learning how to take charge of your car and competently handle its maintenance and general care, you are now perfectly positioned to take the plunge. *Every Woman's Quick & Easy Car Care* will guide you on an exploratory journey that shows you what to do, when to do it, and when you're in over your head and should get help.

For quick reference, the book is divided into six parts:

● **Inside the Car** examines the dashboard console and indicator lights — including what to do when an indicator light comes on — and offers the most up-to-date information available on using safety belts and child-restraint seats.

● **Under the Hood** breaks down each of the mechanical systems that together form the engine, showing you what they look like and giving advice on how to keep them operating at peak performance levels.

● **A Peek Underneath** covers tires, suspension, and brakes. Among other mighty tasks, you'll learn how to read the tread on your tires, how to tell if your brakes or shocks are worn, and what to do about it.

● **Troubleshooting** offers insight as to why your car might be producing odd sounds, smells, or behaviors and the right course of action to correct the problem.

● **On-the-Road Emergencies** provides easy-reference guidelines for all kinds of otherwise terror-inducing situations, such as flat tires, dead batteries, and blinding snowstorms.

● **The Real Lowdown on Detailing** shows you how to keep your car looking like new — and having the maximum resale value.

And in the appendix, you'll find maintenance schedules and records, step-by-step checklists to fill out in the sad event that you have a collision, and even a placard to fill out and leave behind if you happen to damage an unoccupied vehicle.

So, please, take what you read in this handbook and apply it to your car. Oh, and one final point — *Every Woman's Quick & Easy Car Care* will best assist you when it's in your car. Simply place it in the glove compartment or the side pocket of the driver's door so that you can rest assured that it will always be there for you.

Drivers, it's my pleasure serving you!

INSIDE THE CAR

The inside of the modern car is beginning to look like the cockpit of an airplane. Strange-symboled buttons, hidden switches, blinking lights, digital monitors, all piled on top of each other across the dashboard. After just a few excursions, you grow accustomed to the layout of your car's gears — this button is for the headlights, that switch for the windshield wipers, and not the other way around. But then comes the day when you're cruising down Main Street, hair in the wind, carefree and confident, and as you nonchalantly pass your eyes over the dashboard, something catches your attention. A red light. One you've never noticed before. In a long, slow, momentum-gathering second, you wonder, "What is that? How long has it been on? Is that bad? Should I keep going? Do I need to pull over? Is the engine going to clunk out? Will it explode?"

Now your heart leaps. Your stomach clenches. Your hands are suddenly clammy. Panic sets in.

Of course, if you were familiar with the indicator lights on your dashboard, the systems to which they are tied, and what those systems look like under the hood of your car, you might, instead, feel cool as a cucumber — Ms. Calm and Collected in the face of automotive adversity. Oh, what a hassle, you might need a new battery. You might have to bring the car to your mechanic tomorrow. You might have to pull over and call for a tow truck. But whatever you might have to do, you'd feel confident that it's the right decision, for the sake of your car's longevity and your own personal safety. And confidence, my friends, is the key to happy and safe driving.

We'll tackle the systems under the hood in the next chapter. For now, let's start with the controls inside your car, in what is known as the passenger compartment. These are the systems that allow you to drive in comfort and with peace of mind. So strap in — your adventure in car care starts here!

Reading the Dashboard

The indicator lights on your dashboard tell you what's happening under the hood of your car. Indicator lights that are red will come on when something has gone wrong. Indicator lights that are not warnings are not red; the right and left turn signals, for example, are green, and the high-beam headlight indicator is usually blue.

Reading indicator lights is simple. Each red light should come on briefly when you start up your car. After only about five seconds, all red lights should go off. If a light stays on, it means that there may be a problem in its particular area of responsibility. For example, if the oil pressure light stays on, it could be telling you that there isn't enough oil in the engine oil pan.

The dashboard commonly has indicator lights for each of the following:

- "Check engine"
- Battery or charge
- Oil pressure
- Safety belts
- Turn signals
- Braking system
- Cruise control
- High-beam headlights
- Fuel

Your car may have additional indicator lights for features specific to your make and model; check your owner's manual for details.

Gauges to Keep an Eye On

There are two gauges on the dashboard: the temperature gauge and the fuel gauge. The temperature gauge monitors the heat of the engine. The fuel gauge tells you how much gasoline your car has in its tank. All this is, of course, necessary information for the driver. So while you crawl along city streets or cruise down highways and byways, keep an eye on these two gauges.

When you first start up your car, the arrow on the temperature gauge should be in the cold (blue or white) zone. As you drive and the engine warms up, the arrow should slowly rise to about the halfway mark, between the cold zone and the hot (red) zone, and that's where it should stay. If the arrow moves into the red zone, it means that your car's engine is probably overheating.

The proper course of action when your car's engine overheats depends on the rate at which the heat increases.

The dashboard

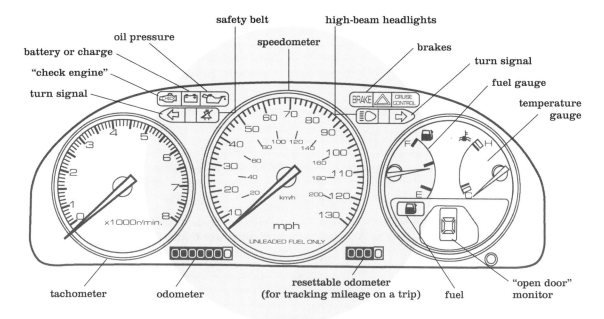

The starring characters on most dashboard consoles are the speedometer, the fuel gauge, and the temperature gauge. Dashboards in manual-transmission vehicles, like this one, also feature a tachometer, which measures the revolutions of the engine. Indicator lights are displayed above these gauges.

AUTOTALK

It's not uncommon for a car to overheat occasionally on very hot days, especially in stop-and-go traffic. However, if your car frequently overheats under less rigorous circumstances, bring it to your mechanic for an evaluation.

If the arrow on the temperature gauge moves slowly toward the hot zone, your engine is not being cooled adequately. To temporarily solve this problem, turn on the heat, letting it run on high. The heater pulls warmth from the engine and releases it into the passenger compartment. This solution may turn the inside of your car into a moving tropical zone, especially if your car happens to overheat in midsummer, but it will help cool the engine, which is what you want to accomplish. Bring the car to your mechanic for an evaluation at your earliest convenience.

If the arrow on the temperature gauge moves quickly to the red zone, some part of the engine is malfunctioning. Immediately pull over and turn the ignition key to "off." Call for a tow truck and have your car brought to your mechanic. Do not attempt to drive the car, because any further engine activity could cause engine failure, which will lead to a hefty repair bill and a car that's out of commission for a few days.

See page 210 for more information about what to do when your car's engine overheats.

Most drivers learn to keep an eye on the fuel gauge as a matter of habit. After all, it can be a bit embarrassing to have to explain to the traffic patrol officer that, no, your car didn't break down; you just forgot to gas it up. But monitoring fuel supply is also a practical component of responsible car care. A mostly empty fuel tank offers space for water crystals to accumulate. If these water crystals are drawn into your car's fuel line, they can cause the car to stall. So as a simple measure of preventive maintenance, fill up the fuel tank whenever the arrow in the fuel gauge drops below the halfway mark.

The Hazard Button

One of the many buttons on the dashboard activates what automotive wizards have termed the *hazard lights*. Upon closer inspection, the hazard lights are actually the right and left turn signal lights; when you press the hazard button (identifiable by the triangular symbol it carries), the turn signals on the front and back of the car begin to blink simultaneously.

There are two reasons to activate the hazard lights.

Car trouble. If your car dies, whether you are stopped in a lane of traffic or parked on the shoulder of a highway, turn on the hazard lights as a warning to other motorists. (And don't sit inside your car when it's disabled, even if you're parked on a shoulder. Get well away from the road and your car. It's not uncommon for an inattentive driver to hit a car that's parked on the side of the road.)

You should also activate the hazard lights if you're driving well below the speed limit (as you might if you have a flat tire and are driving toward the nearest rest area so you can change the tire in a spot that's protected from highway traffic).

Inclement weather. If you're driving in heavy fog and you don't have fog lights, activate your hazard lights. They won't help you see any better, but they will certainly help other drivers see you. The same rule applies to heavy rain, blinding blizzards, and hailstorms. (There's a precautionary lesson here: Don't venture out on the roads when visibility isn't good. Also, if you're on the road when inclement weather starts rolling in, drive to the nearest service station, restaurant, or rest area and wait it out.)

The hazard lights symbol

Climate Control

The automobile can be described as a small room in which you sit as you hurtle — or crawl — through the outside elements. Like a room in a house, it has windows that must be kept clean and clear so that you can see your surrounding environment. The room must also be heated or cooled to a temperature that is comfortable to the human body. For these purposes, the architects of automotive engineering created climate-control units. However great their task, these units are generally easy to use and understand.

Settings on the climate-control units are usually twofold:

The air-recirculation setting recirculates air that is already inside your car. This setting is ideal during the months of extreme temperatures; it keeps the heater working on preheated air and the air conditioner working on precooled air. This setting can also be useful if you drive in heavy traffic; a self-contained air supply helps minimize the amount of exhaust fumes entering your car from other vehicles.

The flow-through setting allows outside air to replace air already inside your car. This setting can also help prevent the inside windows from fogging, even when temperatures are low.

The air-recirculation button

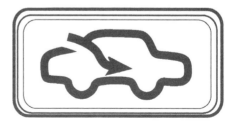

The flow-through button

The Defroster and Heater

As you'll read in part 2, Under the Hood, the heating system of your car allows the heat carried by the engine's cooling system to pass into the passenger compartment. The defroster and heater are a part of the heating system. The defroster works to clear ice and fog from the inside windows of your car, and the heater keeps your fingers and toes warm.

To save added wear and tear on engine parts, let the engine warm up for a couple of minutes before activating the heater or the defroster. This gives engine parts and fluids time to warm up and start working at full efficiency before you draw heat away from them. Once the heater and defroster have been turned on, it should take only about five minutes for the passenger compartment of your car to warm up and the windows to defrost. If it takes any longer, the heater core may be defective.

The rear window in most cars is embedded with horizontal thin metal wires. These wires, combined with an electronic switch at the dashboard, make up the rear window defroster. When you push the rear defroster button on the dashboard to the "on" position, electricity is sent through those thin wires. They, in turn, heat up, melting ice from the outside of the window.

The rear window defroster should turn off automatically after about ten minutes. This is ample time for the window to defrost. If the rear window doesn't clear, either the defroster is malfunctioning or the amount of snow or ice you've asked it to defrost is too much. If the rear window has a thick sheet of ice or snow on it, don't expect the defroster to take care of it all. Get out and scrape first. *Then* hit the rear defroster button. You'll have a clear window more quickly, and by not hitting the rear defroster button over and over again, you'll also extend the life of the rear defroster switch.

Air-Conditioning

Air-conditioning is sheer luxury in warmer regions, where the swampy hot temperatures of summer can be banished with the touch of a button. But air conditioners are best used judiciously. Why? They're tremendous gas guzzlers.

Statistics indicate that a vehicle uses up to 20 percent more fuel when its air-conditioning unit is operating than when it is not.

To reduce fuel consumption, use your air conditioner only when it's absolutely necessary. And open some windows to let hot air inside your car escape before turning it on.

AUTOTALK

If you notice fog coming in through the vents after you turn on the air-conditioning, don't be alarmed. This is simply moist air suddenly turned cold — like the white puff of air that you see when you exhale in cold weather. The fog shouldn't last long. In the meantime, you might want to open your window a crack to clear the air.

Defogging the Windows

Sometimes car windows fog up on the inside, obscuring your vision. This happens when warm, moist air meets a cold window — the moisture in the warm air condenses upon contact, forming little water droplets on the glass. When you're driving around with a car stuffed full of people, the windows tend to fog up even more rapidly, because the body heat of the extra passengers warms the air and their exhalations add more moisture to that air.

The solution is not to ask your passengers to stop breathing. Instead, warm the windows by turning on the defroster or cool the air by turning on the air conditioner. Either device should alleviate the condensation within a few minutes. If you opt for the heat, be sure to use the flow-through setting (see page 8), which allows the warm, moist air in your car to be replaced with fresh air from outside.

For some reason, dirty windows tend to fog up more quickly and more completely than clean ones. To prevent your windows from fogging, wash them on the inside regularly (see page 230).

Safety Belts

In the event of a collision or rollover, the safety belt system cradles you against the seat, confining you to a limited, safe area. Even a minor fender bender can lead to serious injuries if you aren't properly belted in. By securing you in place, the safety belt system also helps you maintain control of your car when, for example, you have to brake suddenly. Instead of being thrown forward and perhaps banging into the steering wheel, you stay secure in your seat and are able to keep an eye on the situation and react accordingly.

For maximum protection, the shoulder and lap belts must be positioned correctly. Fit the shoulder belt across your collarbone and over your chest. Never place the shoulder belt under your arm; in a crash, a belt strapped on in this position could break your ribs, which could result in a punctured heart or lung. Secure the lap belt across your hips (*not* over your waist or lower abdomen). Once you are buckled in, pull up on the shoulder belt until both the lap and shoulder belts are snug.

Every time you clean your car, examine the safety belts for signs of wear and tear. Twisted belts should be untwisted; frayed belts need to be replaced to be fully effective. Check the belt buckles, as well. Dirt, food particles, and other grime lodged in a buckle can cause it to malfunction.

The shoulder and lap belts should fit snugly against the body. Secure the lap belt across the hips; the shoulder belt should cross over the collarbone and chest.

Seat Positioning

For maximum protection in the event of a collision, it's important to wear the shoulder and lap belts *and* to have the seat and the steering wheel in the correct position.

Many nervous drivers, especially those of shorter stature, pull their seat much too close to the dashboard, perhaps feeling that being right up next to the steering wheel and brakes will give them better control of the car. This is not true. In fact, it's downright dangerous. Even a minor collision can lead to injury if you're sitting too close to the steering wheel and air bag. Instead, follow these simple guidelines:

1 Move your seat as far back as you can while still being able to reach the brake and gas pedals comfortably. Your chest should be 10 to 12 inches (25–30 cm) from the steering wheel.

2 Position the seat in a slightly reclining position.

3 Tilt the steering wheel down so that its top is below your chin.

Improper seat position

Proper seat position

Move the seat away from the steering wheel, recline the seat slightly, tilt the steering wheel down, and fasten the safety belts to achieve proper seat positioning.

Safety Belts During Pregnancy

In a collision, *not* wearing a safety belt exposes the fetus to greatest harm. What if the mother is ejected from the car? What if she is thrown against the steering wheel? The safety belt system protects both the mother and her unborn baby from injury.

If you're pregnant, wear the lap belt across your hips. Draw the shoulder belt down between your breasts and snugly above the top of your belly. Do not wear the lap belt or shoulder belt across your belly; you don't want to apply any undue pressure — from a collision or even braking — to the womb.

Minimize your time behind the wheel during the last three months of pregnancy, as your belly (and baby) will sit dangerously close to the steering wheel.

A pregnant woman should wear the lap belt over the hips and the shoulder belt over the collarbone, between the breasts, and above — not across — the belly.

No Excuse Is a Good Excuse

People have plenty of reasons for not wearing a safety belt. When examined objectively, however, none of them makes much sense. So when your friends or family offer up these excuses for not wearing a safety belt, set them straight.

I'm a good driver. I'm not going to get into a collision. The merits of this particular excuse are subject to discussion, and in any case, you're not the only one on the road. There are plenty of bad or distracted drivers out there, and sometimes you just can't avoid them. And safety belts offer more than just protection. Research has shown that they also prevent fatigue by keeping the user from slouching.

Whether or not I wear a safety belt is my own business. It's not just your business — it's the law. If you have children, it's even more important to wear a safety belt. Children learn by imitating. When they see you buckle up, they'll do so themselves.

Safety belts will trap me in the car if I'm in a collision. It's been proved that wearing a safety belt improves your chances of surviving a collision. You sometimes hear miraculous stories of a passenger not wearing a safety belt who was thrown from a car during a collision and survived. Well, these are indeed miracles. Statistics show that if you're thrown from a vehicle, you're four times as likely to end up dead or permanently disabled.

My kids complain about having to wear safety belts. It's easier to give in than to argue. If a child complains about having to wear a safety belt, perhaps she's too small for it. If, for example, the shoulder belt chafes against your daughter's neck, she should be sitting in a booster seat. She's too small for a regular safety belt. For full riding comfort as well as maximum protecion, children who cannot pass the five-step test (see page 25) should use a safety seat appropriate for their size.

Air Bags

Dual frontal air bags are now a standard feature in automobiles. The driver's air bag sits inside the steering wheel; the passenger's air bag fits in the dashboard. Some cars also have side air bags installed in the side of the seats or in the car doors.

When the car stops suddenly, electronic sensors tell the air bags to deploy. Most air bags deploy at speeds of up to 200 mph (330 kph). Some newer vehicles are equipped with "dual-speed" air bags, which deploy with 20 to 35 percent less force than single-speed air bags. This is a great innovation for shorter drivers (under 5'4" or 160 cm) who must sit closer to the steering wheel.

Although air bags are a tremendously effective safety mechanism, they can cause broken wrists, broken ribs, and whiplash in passengers who are improperly positioned. That's another reason why it's important to position your seat properly. See page 12 for details. In addition, if there is a passenger air bag, *never* use a rear-facing child safety seat in the front seat, and have children under the age of 13 sit in the backseat whenever possible.

Child Safety Seats

Automobiles are designed for the comfort and safety of adults, not children. So when you travel with kids as passengers, you must make accommodations for them. There are two very important rules to keep in mind:

1 Children under the age of 13 should ride in the backseat.

2 Until children can pass the five-step test (see page 25), they need to ride in a child safety seat.

Why do kids have to sit in the back? First, the backseat is the safest spot in an automobile. Second, the air bag for the front passenger seat, when deployed, can injure or kill a small child.

Child safety seats are a top priority for young passengers. Children need the extra protection of a safety seat until they are big enough to fit properly in lap and shoulder belts.

Finding a seat that is appropriate for your child can be a confusing process. There are as

AUTOTALK

When you are installing a child safety seat in your car, kneel on the seat to make sure that it is pressed firmly against the car's seat back before tightening the safety belts that hold it in place.

many makes and models of child safety seats as there are makes and models of cars. The challenge is to purchase a safety seat that is appropriate for your child's age and size and that fits properly in the backseat of your particular vehicle.

There are five basic types of child safety seats:

- Infant-only seats
- Convertible seats
- Built-in and other forward-facing-only seats
- Combination seats (part safety seat, part booster)
- Booster seats

Infant-Only Safety Seats

Infant-only safety seats are suitable for babies up to about nine months of age. Most are easy to remove from the backseat of your car and serve a dual purpose as both a carrier and a child safety seat.

Secure the infant in the seat before placing it in the backseat of your car. Adjust the harness to make sure that the shoulder straps lie flat across the front of the child. Adjust the chest clip so that it is level with the infant's armpits. Make sure the harness fits snugly. If you are able to pinch a tuck in the fabric of the harness between your fingers, it is too loose.

When you install the infant safety seat in your car, place it facing the rear of your car and, if possible, in the middle of the backseat. The baby should recline at about a 45-degree angle. Most infant safety seats have a removable base that can be buckled securely into the vehicle using the safety belt system and left in place; the seat then snaps into the base. Most infant safety seats also may be used without the base. Follow the instructions of the safety seat's manufacturer and the instructions in your vehicle's owner's manual for proper installation.

Once your baby and the safety seat are secured, lock the carrying handle by folding it down over an end of the seat; don't leave it extended over the baby's head. Finally, cover your baby with whatever blankets are necessary to keep her warm.

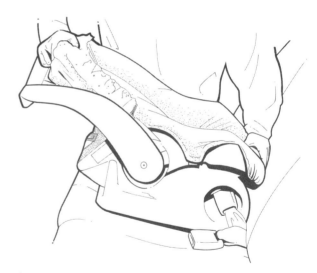

If your infant safety seat has a detachable base, you can leave it in the backseat of your car on a permanent basis. When it's time to take the baby for a ride, the seat snaps into the base.

Your baby will require a larger safety seat before her head reaches within an inch of the top edge of the seat or before she reaches the maximum weight specified by the seat's manufacturer.

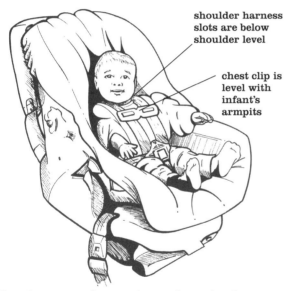

shoulder harness slots are below shoulder level

chest clip is level with infant's armpits

This infant is properly secured in an infant-only safety seat; she is cradled comfortably, well supported, and protected from harm. Make it a habit of running through the checklist at right every time you buckle your baby into the seat.

Infant Safety Seat Checklist

☐ Safety seat is in the backseat (preferably the middle) of the vehicle, facing the rear.

☐ Safety seat is installed according to the instructions provided by the manufacturer and your vehicle's owner's manual.

☐ Safety seat cannot be moved more than an inch (2.5 cm) toward the front or sides of the vehicle.

☐ Shoulder harness slots are at or below the infant's shoulders

☐ Chest retainer clip is level with infant's armpits.

☐ Harness is snug; you cannot "pinch" together any slack.

☐ Safety seat is tilted back to a 45-degree angle so that the infant's head does not flop forward. (If the seat is not tilted back sufficiently, tuck a rolled-up towel under its front edge to tip it back further.)

Convertible Child Safety Seats

Convertible child safety seats can be used in both rear- and forward-facing positions, offering parents an infant seat and toddler seat in one unit. They have lower shoulder harness slots for babies and higher slots for toddlers. There are three harness types: the five-point harness, the harness with abdominal T-shield, and the harness with tray shield. The five-point harness is preferable; for newborns, it's essential.

The convertible child safety seat *must* be used in a rear-facing position until your baby is at least one year old *and* weighs 22 pounds (10 kg). It's safer to keep her in the rear-facing position for as long as possible; most convertible seats are certified up to 30 pounds (14 kg) for the rear-facing position. Review the owner's manual for your child's safety seat to find out what weight it is certified for. When you do use the seat in a forward-facing position, move the shoulder straps to the top harness slots.

WHICH SEAT FOR WHICH KID?

Child	Age Range	Weight Range	Type of Seat
Infant	Birth to 1 year	Up to about 22 lbs (10 kg)	Rear-facing infant-only or convertible child safety seat
Toddler	Age 1 and up	22 to 40 lbs (10–18 kg)	Rear-facing for as long as possible; then forward-facing child safety seat or combination child seat–booster seat
Young child	Age 3 and up	40 to 80 lbs (18–36 kg)	Belt-positioning booster or a safety seat with certified high-weight straps until the child passes the five-step test on page 25.

Convertible seat harnesses

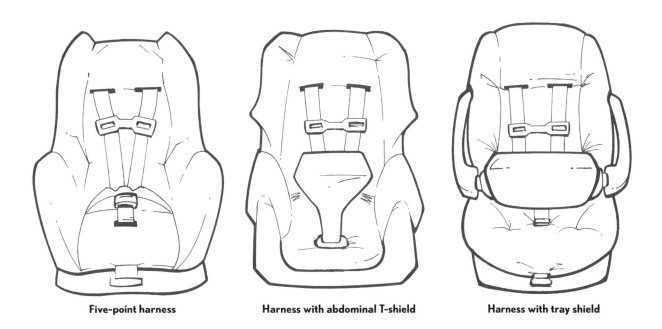

Five-point harness   Harness with abdominal T-shield   Harness with tray shield

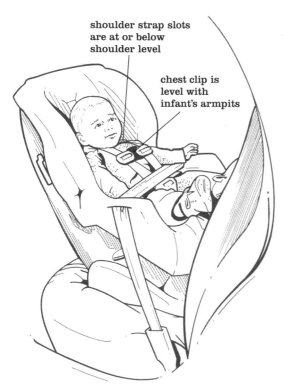

shoulder strap slots are at or below shoulder level

chest clip is level with infant's armpits

For infants, the convertible child safety seat should be used in a rear-facing position. The shoulder straps should be fed through the lower slots, which are at or below the child's shoulders.

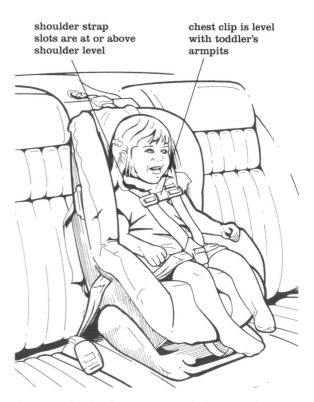

shoulder strap slots are at or above shoulder level

chest clip is level with toddler's armpits

When your child is at least one year old, she may sit facing forward in the convertible seat. Now the shoulder straps should be fed through the top harness slots, which must be at or above the child's shoulders.

Convertible Child Safety Seat Checklist

For All Users

☐ Seat is secured in the backseat, preferably in the center.

☐ Seat is installed according to the instructions provided by the manufacturer and your vehicle's owner's manual.

☐ Chest retainer clip is level with the child's armpits.

☐ Harness is snug; you cannot "pinch" together any slack.

☐ Blankets or other bulky coverings are laid on top of the secured child, not buckled in with her.

For Babies

☐ Seat faces the rear.

☐ Seat is tilted back to a 45-degree angle so that the infant's head does not flop forward.

☐ Shoulder straps are fed through the lower slots, which are at or below the child's shoulders.

For Toddlers

☐ Child is at least one year old.

☐ Child weighs at least 22 pounds (10 kg).

☐ Seat faces forward.

☐ Shoulder straps are fed through the top slots, which should be above the child's shoulders. (If the slots are above the ears, the child should still be in the rear-facing position.)

Built-In Child-Restraint Seats

Some vehicles — particularly minivans — have built-in child safety seats. When you flip down a panel in the back support of the backseat, a child safety seat appears and locks itself in place. This type of child safety seat can be incredibly convenient and make your travel arrangements versatile, but first you must make sure that your child fits safely and comfortably in the seat. See the checklist below. Keep in mind that these seats are suitable for children who are over the age of one *and* weigh at least 22 pounds (10 kg).

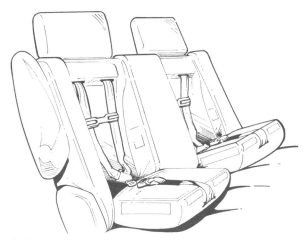

Built-in child-restraint seats relieve you of the hassle of always having one seat occupied by a child's car seat. Adult passengers can simply fold the child-restraint seat into the seat back. If the built-in seat isn't safe and comfortable for your child, however, forgo the convenience and install a traditional child safety seat for her.

Built-In Seat Checklist for Toddlers

☐ Toddler is at least one year old.

☐ Toddler weighs more than 22 pounds (10 kg) but less than the weight limit given by the manufacturer, which can be found in your vehicle's owner's manual.

☐ Slots for the shoulder straps are at or above the toddler's shoulders.

☐ Chest retainer clip is level with the child's armpits.

☐ Harness is snug; you cannot "pinch" together any slack.

Combination Child Seats–Boosters

Combination seats face forward and have a removable harness. They are sometimes called high-backed boosters with a built-in harness. If your child is at least three years old and outgrows the harness, remove it and use the seat as a booster with the vehicle's lap and shoulder belts. If your child is too heavy or tall for the combination seat but is still under the age of three, you'll have to look for a different option.

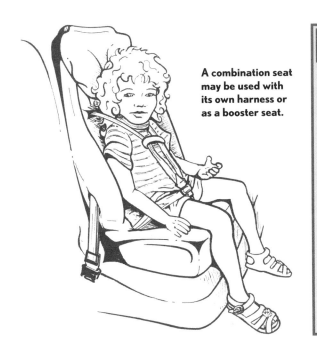

A combination seat may be used with its own harness or as a booster seat.

Combination Seat Checklist

☐ Child is at least one year old and within the weight range specified for the seat.

☐ Seat is secured in the backseat, facing forward.

☐ Seat is installed according to the instructions provided by the manufacturer and your vehicle's owner's manual.

☐ Shoulder harness slots are at or above the child's shoulders.

☐ Chest retainer clip is level with the child's armpits.

☐ Harness is snug; you cannot "pinch" together any slack.

Booster Seats

A booster seat raises your child so that the vehicle's shoulder and lap belts fit safely and securely across her chest and hips. Boosters are a transition step between a child safety seat with a full harness and the vehicle's safety belt system.

Boosters are suitable for children who are at least three years old and have outgrown a safety seat with a harness. There are two types:

① **Backless belt-positioning boosters** lift the child up to a position where the vehicle's safety belts fit properly.

② **High-back belt-positioning boosters** must be used in vehicles that have low seat backs or no headrests. If the child's ears rise above the top of the backseat, this type of booster is necessary to support his head and protect his neck.

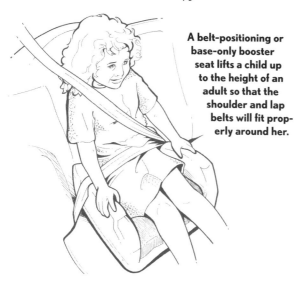

A belt-positioning or base-only booster seat lifts a child up to the height of an adult so that the shoulder and lap belts will fit properly around her.

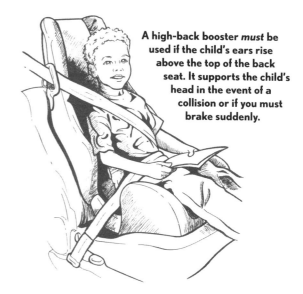

A high-back booster *must* be used if the child's ears rise above the top of the back seat. It supports the child's head in the event of a collision or if you must brake suddenly.

The Five-Step Test

Did you know that most kids need to ride in a booster seat from about the age of four until at least the age of eight? If your child falls within this age range and isn't using a booster, try this simple test, devised by SafetyBeltSafe U.S.A. (www.carseat.org), the next time you ride together in the car.

1 Does your child sit all the way back against the auto seat?

2 Do the child's knees bend comfortably at the edge of the auto seat?

3 Does the belt cross the shoulder between the neck and the arm?

4 Is the lap belt as low as possible, touching the thighs?

5 Can the child stay seated like this for the entire trip?

Booster Seat Checklist

☐ Child is at least three years old.

☐ Booster is installed according to the instructions provided by the manufacturer and your vehicle's owner's manual.

☐ If the child's ears rise above top of backseat, the booster seat has a high back.

☐ Lap belt fits across the child's hips.

☐ Shoulder belt fits across the child's collarbone and chest.

If you answered "no" to any of these questions, your child needs a booster to ride safely in the car. You'll find that your child enjoys the booster because it's more comfortable.

The LATCH/ISOFIX Revolution

Child safety seats come in many different sizes and designs. Safety belt systems in passenger cars and light trucks have a multitude of possible configurations. Putting the two together is often a difficult task. Studies have shown that up to 95 percent of child safety seats are misused in some way, and much of the blame for that can be attributed to the difficulty involved in installing them correctly.

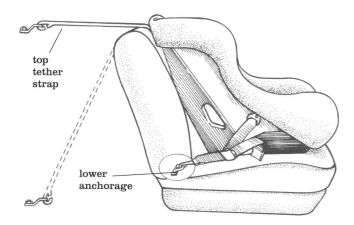

The LATCH/ISOFIX system should reduce misuse of child safety seats by standardizing and simplifying installation.

Thankfully, a tremendous revolution is under way. Manufacturers of child safety seats and manufacturers of motor vehicles are cooperating with various agencies and governments throughout the world to standardize the installation design of child safety seats. As of the year 2002, all new passenger cars feature at least two seating positions with a child restraint anchorage system, consisting of two lower anchorages and one upper anchorage that allow the installation of a child safety seat independent of the vehicle's safety belt system. These three anchorage points correspond to three-point attachment hardware featured on most new child safety seats.

In the United States, the term for this new three-point system is LATCH (*L*ower *A*nchors and *T*ethers for *CH*ildren). In Canada and Europe, the term is ISOFIX (*I*nternational *S*tandards *O*rganization *FIX*). While there are some minor differences between the LATCH and ISOFIX systems, the concept remains the same: fixed anchorage points for child safety seats that allow you to install the seat in the backseat of a passenger vehicle more easily.

The three-point attachment system on a child safety seat consists of a top tether and two lower attachments. The top tether secures the top of the child safety seat to the vehicle; it runs from the top of the safety seat to an anchorage found on the rear shelf of passenger cars or on the floor or ceiling of minivans, some SUVs, pickup trucks, and other vehicles. The two lower attachments connect to anchorages secured in the crack between the seat cushion and the seat back of the vehicle's backseat.

Installing a child safety seat in a new vehicle, then, is a simple matter of securing the three attachments on the seat to their corresponding anchorages in the vehicle. Kneel on the child seat to make sure it is pressed against the vehicle seat back, tighten the attachments, and the seat is secured.

The new LATCH/ISOFIX systems don't use the vehicle's safety belt system. However, this doesn't mean that child safety seats that *are* secured by the safety belt system are not safe. Safety belt–secured seats are just as safe as LATCH/ISOFIX child-restraint seats, provided they are properly installed. The new system just simplifies the installation process.

Checking for a Recall

Although all manufacturers of child safety seats put their seats through rigorous testing, there are occasionally design flaws that go unnoticed until many hundreds or thousands of a particular make and model of child safety seat have been sold. In such cases, the government mandates that the manufacturer of the safety seat initiate a recall.

Of course, the manufacturer of a child safety seat can't notify you about the recall unless you notify it that you've purchased the seat. That's why it's important to fill out and mail in the registration card that comes with a new child safety seat.

You can find out on your own whether there's been a recall of a particular make and model of child safety seat. The U.S. National Highway Traffic Safety Administration (www.nhtsa.gov) offers up-to-date listings of child safety seats that have been recalled. And SafetyBeltSafe U.S.A. (www.carseat.org) offers a list of child safety seats that have recognized problems but have not been recalled; their Web site will tell you whether the manufacturer of a particular seat is offering replacement parts.

UNDER THE HOOD

Having a well-running car that will always get you from here to there and saving on costly repair bills are strong incentives for taking the plunge and getting to know what sits where under the hood. Even if you have no desire to get down and dirty with the engine, it's good sense to know how to check the engine oil, which spout you're supposed to pour the windshield washer fluid into, and why a few particularly stubborn gears and cogs are the usual suspects when your car won't start.

Your car's engine is unique to the make and model of your particular car. It may look a bit different from the engines in other cars — or even the engines illustrated in this book — but overall you'll find more similarities than differences. What's most important is that you get to know what's under the hood of *your* car, rather than examining someone else's engine or looking only at the illustrations herein.

Take this book out to the garage or driveway, pop open the hood, and start identifying the different components as you read about them. There's no better way to get to know the cogs and gears of your car's engine, how they work together to keep the engine running smoothly, and how to tell when they need to be repaired or replaced. Best of all, you'll learn how to perform some of the very simple maintenance tasks that will keep your car in great shape for years to come. You may not become a mechanic overnight, but you will gain confidence in fiddling with this and tinkering with that, in filling that up and wiping this down, in fixing one thing yourself and bringing the car to your mechanic to evaluate something else. Your mechanical knowledge and skills will increase, but it's your newfound confidence you'll treasure most. There's no reason to be afraid of automotive adversity — once you know what's what under the hood. That's what this chapter is all about.

Popping Open the Hood

This may sound like a silly question, but do you know where the hood latch is inside your car? Of course you probably do, but if you don't, get out your owner's manual and find out where the latch is. The latch is usually imprinted with a small symbol of a car with its hood partly open, and it is usually located just under the dashboard, to the left of the driver's seat. When you pull the latch, the hood unlocks, opening to a position that is just slightly ajar.

Walk around to the front of the car and slide your fingers underneath the hood. Feel around for the safety release lever. In most cars, this lever is at the center of the hood, and to release it you must push it up or pull it toward you. You'll hear a metallic popping sound, and now you'll be able to raise the hood.

Some hoods stay open on their own, while others must be propped open with a long metal support rod that is usually found lying flat along the front grille. If you think your hood is one that will stay open on its own, check your owner's manual for confirmation; you don't want to assume that the hood will stay open by itself only to have it slam down on your head while you're leaning over the engine. If you must prop your hood open, pry loose the long metal support rod, then take a look at the underside of the hood. It will have many small openings in it, but one in particular will be marked as the right spot to hook the long metal rod into.

Practice finding the safety release lever under the hood a few times, until you know exactly where it is and how to use it. Being able to open the hood quickly saves you frustration later on, such as when you're standing out in a cold rain struggling to open the hood so you can see where all that steam is coming from.

Some cars have hoods that can be opened directly from the outside — there's no interior hood release latch. If you have a car like this, you might consider investing in a hood lock, which can prevent a would-be thief from tampering with the engine or disabling the alarm system. These locks are inexpensive and can be found at most auto parts stores.

Hood support rod

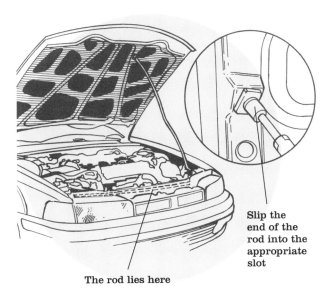

The rod lies here

Slip the end of the rod into the appropriate slot

To prop open the hood, pry loose the long metal rod that lies across the front lip of the engine compartment and secure it to the underside of the hood.

Before You Jump In

Before getting into the fun of inspecting the engine in your car, follow these simple safety guidelines:

- If you have long hair, tie it back.
- Remove all jewelry, including watches and rings.
- Keep a fire extinguisher handy.
- If you're working in a garage, keep the garage door open for ventilation.
- Once the engine is exposed, put on a pair of plastic gloves to keep your hands free of grease.
- Engine fluids such as coolant are poisonous. Store all fluids in a child- and pet-proof location, and wash your hands thoroughly after looking under the hood.
- Never smoke around an open hood when the engine is idling. A stray spark can ignite in the engine, causing a fire.
- Never discount the value of the buddy system for inspiring confidence. Engage the help of a family member or friend anytime you work under the hood.

The Engine Block

Now that you have it open, it's time to poke your head under the hood. Do you see that big blocky thing in the middle of the engine? That's the engine block (also known as the cylinder block). It's encased in cast iron or aluminum, and inside that casing are various components that work together to ignite the engine and keep it running. Of course, because the engine block is encased in metal, you can't see most of those components. But in the safe confines of these pages, we'll take a short tour of the innards of the engine block.

The Cylinders

Vehicles can have four, six, or eight cylinders, although most passenger cars have just four. (The more cylinders your car has, the more power it has. You'll soon see why.) A cylinder is a hollow tube that is closed at the top and open at the bottom. The top of the cylinder (the cylinder head) sits directly below the fuel-injection system (a component we'll discuss shortly). Each cylinder head is fitted with an intake manifold and intake valve, an exhaust mani-fold and exhaust valve, and a spark plug. The intake manifold and intake valve direct fuel into the cylinder; the exhaust manifold and exhaust valve funnel fumes from the cylinder to the exhaust system.

Most cars use gasoline as fuel. Once gas reaches the engine, it's combined with air to form a vapor that burns readily. This fuel vapor finds its way (through the fuel-injection system or, if you have an older car, the carburetor) into the top of the cylinder.

A piston fits snugly inside each cylinder. The piston moves up and down, quite rapidly, inside the cylinder. As the piston moves up, it traps fuel vapor in the cylinder head, compressing it. Now the electrical system gets involved. A spark plug is mounted on top of each cylinder. Through an intricate timing system, the spark plug is "sparked" at the exact moment that the fuel vapor is compressed by the piston in a cylinder. The spark ignites the fuel vapor. The result is a small but powerful explosion that pushes the piston down with considerable force.

The up-and-down movement of the four (or more) pistons in your car's cylinders is timed so that the explosions happen in rapid succession. All the pistons are connected by a rod (aptly called the connecting rod) to the crankshaft. The crankshaft, the main rotating part of the engine block, is connected at its other end to the crankcase.

There are additional parts to the crankcase, such as the cams, springs, valves, and oil pan (you'll want to remember that this is where the oil pan sits — at the bottom of the crankcase), but in a nutshell, this is what happens: As each piston is

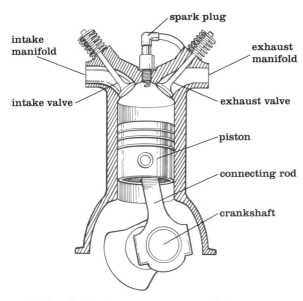

Inside the cylinder, the piston moves up and down, propelled by the force of small explosions sparked by the spark plug in the cylinder head.

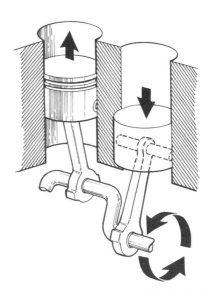

The connecting rods function like the pedals of a bicycle. The pistons move up and down in succession; as one rises, another falls. Their combined momentum turns the crankshaft.

The engine block

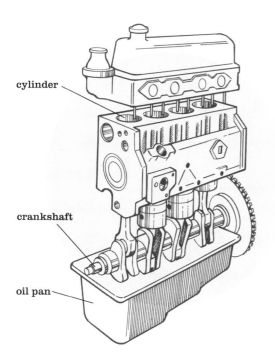

cylinder

crankshaft

oil pan

The cylinders are actually smooth tunnels drilled through the engine block.

forced up and down, it turns the crankshaft, which turns the crankcase, which (eventually) turns the wheels.

Because metal rubs against metal as the pistons pump up and down and the crankcase turns the crankshaft, constant lubrication by the engine oil is needed. This is why it's so important to have a sufficient quantity of clean, high-quality oil in the oil pan. The constant friction of all these fast-moving parts also creates a lot of heat, as you might imagine. The cooling system circulates a water-antifreeze mixture (generically called *coolant*) around the engine block to transfer heat away from all its hot parts. This is why it's also so important to have adequate coolant in the cooling system. You'll read more about engine oil and the coolant later in this section.

More Cylinders = More Power

If you've ever looked at a brochure for a new vehicle, you've seen the engine specifications outlined in big, bold type: "16-valve 6-cylinder engine. Incredible power!" Now that you know how the cylinders work, it's easy to see why having more cylinders means more power. When you have more pistons moving up and down to drive the crankshaft, you can rev up the speed of your wheels more quickly. The result: a car with a lot of get-up-and-go.

Don't allow yourself to get caught up in all this power, though. Six-cylinder cars are great, but guess what? They use more gas than four-cylinder cars. Fuel efficiency is one of the main reasons that most passenger cars have four cylinders. Do you really need all that power? Or would a car with a little less *oomph* but lower fuel costs suit your needs?

Counting Cylinders

If you want to know how many cylinders your car has, you can look up the answer in your owner's manual. But there's also another, quicker way: Simply count the number of spark plug wires extending from your engine block. For example, if your car has four spark plug wires, then it is a four-cylinder engine. Be sure to look on both sides of the engine block; a six-cylinder engine may have three spark plugs on either side of the engine block.

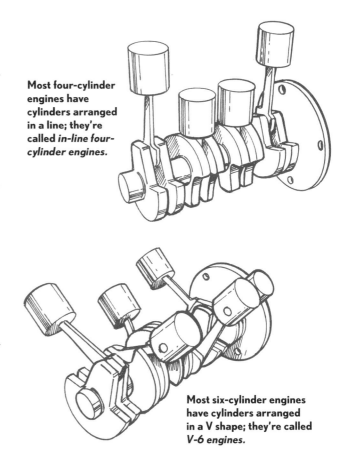

Most four-cylinder engines have cylinders arranged in a line; they're called *in-line four-cylinder engines.*

Most six-cylinder engines have cylinders arranged in a V shape; they're called *V-6 engines.*

The Fuel System

How does gasoline get from the fuel tank to all those cylinders in the engine block? It's actually a simple process, one that Henry Ford developed over one hundred years ago. What has changed over the past decade is the way in which fuel gets *inside* those cylinders. In older cars, a mechanical device called the carburetor combines air and fuel and then distributes the resulting vapor into each cylinder. Since about 1990, however, most car manufacturers have discarded the carburetor in favor of computer-controlled fuel injectors.

What hasn't changed are the five main components of the fuel system: the fuel tank, fuel pump, fuel line, fuel filter, and air filter. The fuel tank houses the gasoline; when you pump gas into your car, you're putting it in the fuel tank. The fuel pump moves gas from the fuel tank through the fuel line to the engine block. Along the way, the gasoline passes through the fuel filter, which removes debris and other impurities.

Now you'll remember that it's not liquid fuel but fuel vapor that is injected into the cylinders.

The fuel system

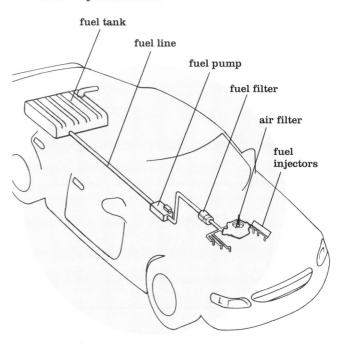

fuel tank

fuel line

fuel pump

fuel filter

air filter

fuel injectors

The fuel system runs the length of the car, bringing gasoline from the tank at the rear to the fuel injectors under the hood.

The air that is combined with the gasoline to form fuel vapor is first passed through the air filter, which sits inside the air cleaner. Purified air meets purified gasoline in the fuel injection system (or carburetor).

The Fuel Pump

A fuel pump does just what you think it might — it pumps fuel. It moves fuel from the fuel tank through the fuel line to the fuel injectors at the engine block.

In some cars, the fuel pump is located inside the fuel tank to prevent *vapor lock* (see page 214). In other cars, the fuel pump is located along the fuel line, between the tank and the engine. If the pump in your car is outside the fuel tank, you can see it by peering underneath the vehicle. Using a flashlight, find the fuel tank and the fuel line that runs from the tank toward the front of the car. Somewhere along the fuel line, you'll see a boxlike or round unit. That's the fuel pump.

Check your owner's manual to find the mileage at which it's recommended that the fuel pump be replaced.

AUTOTALK

One of the most effective and simple ways to keep gasoline properly flowing from the fuel tank to the engine is to keep the tank always at least half full of gas. Why? A mostly empty tank allows water vapor to accumulate inside the tank and along the fuel line. Also, most tanks have a layer of sediment sitting at their bottom; when you're draining the dregs, so to speak, of your gas tank, the gas from the bottom of the tank brings this sediment with it. When you have water or sediment in the fuel system, the engine starts to idle roughly or can even stall.

The Fuel Filter

Given the amount of muck that your car is exposed to, it's easy for fuel to become contaminated. In fact, gasoline can become contaminated with dirt just by sitting in the fuel tank for too long. And that's not counting all the ways fuel can become contaminated before it ever reaches your car, such as when it's drawn from an old underground fuel tank that's rusting away. To keep the engine from running roughly or stalling, your car needs a filtering system to remove impurities from gasoline. That's where the fuel filter comes into play.

The fuel filter can be found under the hood somewhere along the fuel line, most often near the fuel-injection system. It's a metal, plastic, or paper-pleated cylinder, often held together by a clamp on each of its ends. It should be replaced according to the guidelines given in your owner's manual.

The Air Filter

The *air cleaner* is a black metal or plastic container often located beside the fuel-injection system. (In vehicles with carburetors, the air cleaner sits on top of the carburetor.) The air cleaner holds the *air filter,* a screen of pleated sheets of paper. The air filter removes impurities from the air that passes through it; this purified air then mixes with gasoline to form the rich fuel vapor that powers the cylinders.

Some air cleaners are rectangular, others are circular, and still others are cone-shaped. Locate the air cleaner under the hood of your car, noting its shape and how it is secured shut. Some air cleaners are held shut by bolts, while others have small clips.

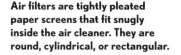

Air filters are tightly pleated paper screens that fit snugly inside the air cleaner. They are round, cylindrical, or rectangular.

Changing the air filter is one of the easiest maintenance tasks you can do on your own — that is, if you can squeeze your hand down through the engine to reach all the clips or bolts that hold the air cleaner shut. It's no wonder some vehicle owner's manuals recommend that a licensed mechanic replace the air filter — sometimes you can't get to it without special tools!

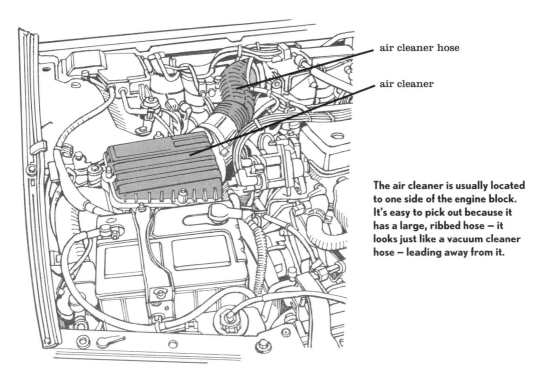

air cleaner hose

air cleaner

The air cleaner is usually located to one side of the engine block. It's easy to pick out because it has a large, ribbed hose — it looks just like a vacuum cleaner hose — leading away from it.

Changing the Air Filter

In the old days, you could check the quality of an air filter by holding it up to the light. If you could see light though the filter, it was still clean enough to continue using. Filters made today, however, can be deceiving. Sometimes they're so thick that no light shines through the paper folds, even though they're quite clean. In general, the air filter should be changed as often as your owner's manual recommends.

TOOLS & SUPPLIES

- Flathead screwdriver (if the air cleaner cover is bolted down)
- New air filter (of the type recommended in your owner's manual)

1 Loosen the air cleaner cover. If the cover of the air cleaner is secured with screws, unscrew them (turning them counterclockwise). If the cover is clamped down by clips, use the head of the screwdriver to snap them open.

2 Remove the top of the air cleaner. The air cleaner cover is usually attached to a large hose,

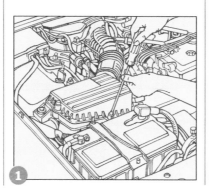

so you can't remove it from the engine completely. Just wiggle it loose and carefully push it out of the way.

3 Examine the position of the air filter. Take a good look at where and how the air filter sits inside the base of the cleaner. When you install the new filter, it should occupy the exact same position.

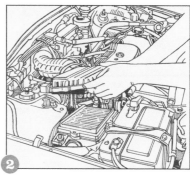

④ Remove the air filter. Using both hands, lift the air filter from the base of the air cleaner.

⑤ Install the new air filter. Take the new air filter out of its packaging. Set it in the air cleaner base in the appropriate position. With the tips of your fingers, push the filter down firmly all around its outer edges to make sure that it fits tight.

⑥ Replace the top of the air cleaner. Set the air cleaner cover on the air cleaner base. Snap on all the clips or reinsert and tighten the screws (turning them clockwise) with the flat-head screwdriver. Double-check that all clips have been reset; it's easy to miss one or two, especially if they're hard to reach.

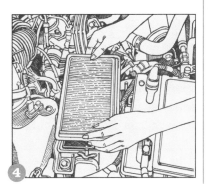

EASY SHOPPING

Because air filters come in a variety of shapes and sizes, check your car owner's manual for the specific part number of the air filter that your car uses. Jot this number down for quick reference in the Vehicle Specifications Record found in the appendix (see page 239). The next time you make a trip to the auto parts store, take the specifications record with you. Whatever you came to buy, whether it be a new air filter or a PCV valve, you'll have at your fingertips the information you need to get the right type for your vehicle.

The Gas Gauge

An important component of the fuel system that you don't often hear about is the fuel tank electronic sending unit. This unit (actually, it's a float ball) tracks the amount of gas in the fuel tank and transmits this information to the gas gauge at the dashboard. If this sending unit becomes defective, the driver receives an inaccurate reading of the amount of fuel in the tank.

While you cannot see the electronic sending unit, because it sits inside the gas tank, you have to run out of gas only once before you realize that the gas gauge is not working.

AUTOTALK

If you find yourself in a situation where you can't get gasoline with the octane rating you've been using, use the next-higher grade (usually premium).

What Type of Gas?

When you pull up to the gas station pump, you're usually presented with a virtual fuel buffet. Which type of gasoline should you use? This question is easily resolved by checking your vehicle's owner's manual. It will tell you which octane rating is best suited for your particular make and model.

Why is this important information for the driver? For the most part, it's important information for your wallet. Most cars are designed to use regular-grade or mid-grade gasoline. There's no need to pay the added expense for premium gas if your car won't benefit from it.

What you should *not* do is switch back and forth between different grades of gasoline. Why? In a fuel-injected car, the computer that controls the rate of fuel injection becomes accustomed to operating with a certain type of gas. Trading grades of gasoline can play havoc with the computer, and as a result, your car may run roughly.

What this boils down to is that you should use the type of gasoline that is recommended by your owner's manual. This habit will save you money in the long run, in both fuel and repair costs.

The Electrical System

What causes the fuel vapor in the cylinder heads to ignite, launching your car into movement? One little spark from each of the spark plugs. And how does a spark plug create that firing power? Electricity, of course.

Electricity is stored in the battery. When you turn the key in the ignition to "start," some of the electricity stored in the battery is sent to the starter solenoid and motor, which jump-start the engine. When you let go of the key and it sinks back to the "on" position, electricity continues to flow through the engine because the alternator, which produces electricity, has been activated.

The alternator is attached by a belt to the crankshaft. (Remember the crankshaft? It sits at the bottom of the engine block and is turned by the pumping movement of each of the pistons inside the cylinder.) As the engine runs, the crankshaft drives the alternator belt, which spins the alternator head and allows the alternator to produce electricity. The electricity it produces is used to recharge the battery and run on-board gadgets such as the radio and windshield wipers. Some of that electricity is also sent to the spark plugs, allowing them to fire. The spark plugs get the pistons moving, and the pistons get the engine cranking, and the engine drives the alternator belt around and around. The alternator belt spins the alternator, which allows it to produce more electricity, and so on. It's an ongoing cycle.

The alternator is controlled by the voltage regulator, which keeps the electrical current produced by the alternator at a manageable level and flow. On newer cars, the voltage regulator is mounted inside the alternator, where you'll never see it.

The electrical system

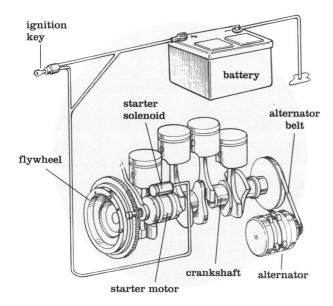

When you turn the key in the ignition, the starter motor comes on. It powers the flywheel, which turns the crankshaft, which gets the pistons moving. The crankshaft drives the alternator belt, which allows the alternator to spin and produce electricity.

The Battery

In most cars, the battery is one of the more obvious components under the hood. If you don't spot it at first glance, your owner's manual should tell you where it is.

On top of the battery are two posts, one for positive current and one for negative current. How can you tell which is which? The positive post is usually marked with a + symbol and the negative post with a – symbol. Also, the positive post is sometimes a bit larger than the negative post.

Two cables extend from the two battery posts. Follow each of the cables to see where it ends. The cable connected to the positive post usually leads to the starter and the starter solenoid. The negative cable leads to the frame of the car — it grounds the circuit of electricity. In many cars the battery cables are color-coded: The positive cable is red and the negative cable is black.

Batteries in most passenger cars are wet-cell, meaning that they're filled with an electrolyte fluid (acid and distilled water). A wet-cell battery is divided into compartments, called cells. Each cell contains a group of metal plates. The plates are made up of different kinds of metal, and in the electrolyte solution they lose electrons to each other. This flow of electrons — otherwise known as electricity — gives the battery its charge.

Some batteries have small vent caps that give you access to the battery's insides. You can't reach down into the battery. (And who'd want to? That's some pretty caustic stuff!) But you can remove the caps and peek inside to see if the plates are deteriorating or if the electrolyte level is low.

Many new car batteries are labeled MAINTENANCE FREE. These batteries are, as promised, long lasting, but they don't relieve you of all battery-related responsibilities. Some maintenance-free batteries don't have any removable vent caps; they're sealed. If this is your situation, you won't be able to check the interior of the battery to determine its condition. However, you can monitor the battery charge, because sealed maintenance-free batteries usually feature an indicator

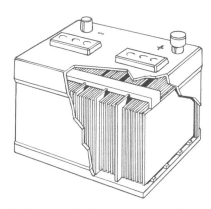

The acid solution inside the battery causes the metal plates to react to one another, creating an electrical charge.

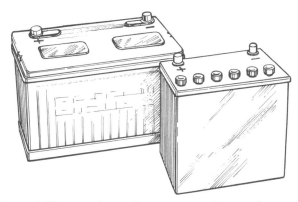

Nonsealed batteries have either two rectangular caps that each cover three compartments or a small removable cap for each compartment.

eye. When the eye is green or yellow, the battery is fully charged. When the eye is black, the battery is discharged.

Like the small batteries that you use in your home to power flashlights, alarm clocks, and hand-held electronic games, a car battery can become discharged — that is, lose all its juice. How does a battery become discharged? There are three main causes:

1 **Accessory drainage.** You park the car and turn off the engine (shutting down the alternator) but leave electrical accessories operating, such as the radio and the headlights. The accessories drain the battery of electricity, and because the alternator isn't resupplying the battery with more electricity, it soon becomes discharged.

2 **Defective electrical circuit.** The battery is not receiving adequate amounts of electricity, as might happen when battery cables are loose, the battery posts and cable ends are dirty, or the alternator belt is loose.

3 **Defective battery.** The battery has lost some of its capacity to store electricity, as may be the case when its electrolyte levels are low, its plates have begun to disintegrate, or it has a current leakage through the plates or a cracked case. You can refill a battery with distilled water (see page 48 for details), but if its plates or case is damaged, it's officially dead — you'll have to have it replaced.

CAUTION

If you need to touch the battery or battery cables, first remove all jewelry. There's a lot of electricity flowing through the cables, even when your car is not running. If anything metal comes in contact with the battery or cables, a shock could result.

If your battery is discharged, you'll have to recharge it — that is, boost or jump-start it. (See page 207 to find out how.)

If your battery is dead, you won't be able to recharge it and you'll have to get a new one. You can either buy a new battery and install it yourself or have the car towed to your mechanic's garage and ask her to replace it.

If you install a new battery yourself, in most cases you'll want to purchase one that is of the same size and rating as the old battery. Check your owner's manual for exact specifications. In some cases it may be advantageous to purchase a battery of a higher rating than that of your current battery. For example, if you keep your cell phone constantly plugged into the cigarette lighter, your electrical system might need a bit of an extra boost from the battery. Talk to your mechanic or a service center representative about this possibility.

To dispose of the dead battery, take it to a service station or automotive center. Batteries contain toxic materials and should never be tossed out with the trash. Service stations and automotive centers have appropriate methods for disposing of old batteries. You may have to pay a station or service center a nominal fee for disposal of your dead battery if you do not also purchase a new battery there.

AUTOTALK

Your battery may become discharged if you haven't driven your car for an extended period of time. Some accessories in your car remain live even after the ignition is turned off, and they slowly suck the energy right out of the battery. It's called parasitic overload. If you anticipate not driving your car for a while, disconnect the battery cables to prevent the battery from becoming discharged. (And remember: Always disconnect the negative cable first.)

Topping Off the Battery

Check the level of the electrolyte periodically, because insufficient electrolyte can lead to a discharged battery. If the electrolyte levels are low, you can top off the battery. (If your battery is sealed, you won't be able to perform this maintenance task.)

Be sure that the car is parked on level ground and the engine is completely cool before you begin this task.

1 **Remove the lock-down case.** If the vent caps on your battery are obstructed by the lock-down case, use a wrench to loosen the case bolts and remove it.

2 **Fill the water bottle.** Fill the bottle with distilled water. (It's important that the water is distilled; tap water contains contaminants that can damage the battery.)

3 **Put on the rubber gloves.** These protect your hands from the caustic electrolyte.

4 **Open a vent cap.** Use the flathead screwdriver to pry off the cap if necessary. Look inside the cell that's revealed. The liquid should be even with the tops of the metal plates inside the battery — never above or below.

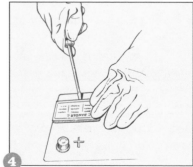

5 Add water. Carefully pour water from the bottle into the vent hole. Try not to splash, and keep an eye on the water level — it doesn't take much to fill a cell.

6 Replace the vent cap. If the vent cap sealed just one cell in the battery, put it back on now and screw it tightly into place. If the cap covered more than one cell, continue to the next step.

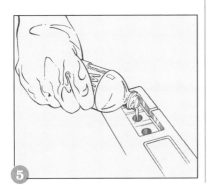

7 Repeat for the other cells. Check, top off, and seal the remaining cells in the battery. Not every cell may need to be topped off.

8 Wipe clean. Once all the cells have been checked, replenished with distilled water, and securely sealed, use a clean rag to wipe away any spilled liquid from the top of the battery.

9 Dispose of materials. Remove the rubber gloves and place them, along with the rag, in a garbage bag. Dispose of the bag in a covered garbage barrel.

LOOK FIRST

If the battery in your car has become discharged more than once over the past couple of weeks, it may be "running on fumes," so to speak. Take a close look at it. Small whiffs of smoke rising from the top of the battery signal that the battery is emitting gases. If you see this smoke, don't top off or jump-start your battery — those gases can be explosive. Instead, replace the battery immediately.

Cleaning the Battery

It's not uncommon for crusty white buildup to appear on the ends of battery cables. If that's what you see when you look at your battery, it's time to clean it — that acid buildup can interfere with the flow of electricity to and from the battery. Give yourself at least an hour for this simple task; there isn't much to it, but you'll want to allow the cables to dry completely after you've cleaned them before you reconnect them to the battery.

Some batteries have lock-down cases that hold them securely in place; others do not. For the sake of those whose batteries are locked down, we'll assume that you'll remove the lock-down case before you can access the battery components.

TOOLS & SUPPLIES

- 1 tablespoon (15 ml) baking soda
- 1 cup (250 ml) warm water
- Small plastic container
- Rubber gloves
- Wrenches (of the right size for the lock-down bolts and cable fittings on your battery)
- Old toothbrush
- Petroleum jelly or battery terminal grease
- Clean rag

1 **Prepare the cleaning solution.** Mix together 1 tablespoon (15 ml) of baking soda with 1 cup (250 ml) of warm water in a small plastic container.

2 **Put on rubber gloves.** These protect your hands from the caustic electrolyte.

3 **Unscrew the lock-down case.** Use a wrench of the appropriate size to loosen the bolts of the case and remove it.

4 **Unscrew the negative cable nut.** Use a wrench of the appropriate size to loosen the nut that clamps the negative cable in place on the battery post.

5 **Remove the negative cable.** Once the battery cable is loose, remove it from the battery post. You may need to wiggle it around to pull it off.

6 **Remove the positive cable.** In the same manner, loosen and pull off the positive cable.

7 **Clean the posts and cable ends.** Dip the toothbrush into the baking soda solution and use it to scrub both posts and

the ends of the cables. Redip as necessary.

8 **Dry.** Allow the cables and posts to dry completely. (This is a nice time to take a break and enjoy a cup of coffee or an ice-cold drink.)

9 **Lubricate.** Smear petroleum jelly or battery terminal grease over the posts and the cable ends.

10 **Reconnect the battery cables.** Connect the positive cable first, screwing it on securely. Then connect the negative cable.

11 **Wipe down.** Use a clean rag to wipe down the top of the battery.

12 **Dispose of materials.** Place the gloves, plastic container, and toothbrush in a bag and dispose of it in a covered garbage barrel.

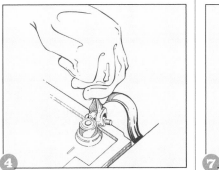

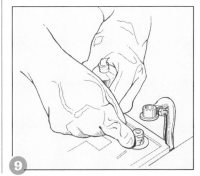

The Starter

The starter is an electrical motor usually located at the bottom and side of the crankshaft. If you follow the path of a battery cable (usually the positive one) from the battery, it will lead you to the starter solenoid — a small cylinder on top of the starter. (In newer cars, the starter solenoid is sometimes incorporated into the starter, where you can't see it.) The solenoid functions as a switch that allows electricity from the battery to reach the starter moter. The starter gets the crankshaft turning, which starts the pistons pumping, the electricity running, and the engine purring.

The Ignition System

When you turn your key to the "start" position, you activate the starting system. When you release the key and it slips back to the "on" position, the ignition system takes over. The ignition system ignites, or fires, the spark plugs and gets your car in motion.

The classic ignition system is made up of four parts: the battery, the ignition coil, the distributor, and the spark plugs. The battery supplies the electricity. The ignition coil amplifies it. The distribu-

tor, naturally, distributes it, in the right amount and at the right time. The spark plugs fire when they receive it.

There are three types of ignition systems: breaker-point ignitions, breakerless ignition systems, and distributorless ignition systems. Older cars with carburetors have a breaker-point ignition system, with a mechanically operated distributor and coil — no electronics. Vehicles with a breakerless ignition system have the classic distributor and coil, but they're controlled by an electronic switch. Most vehicles built today have a distributorless ignition system, which consists of an electronic coil, sensors, and an electronic filter; this new technology replaces the traditional distributor and coil.

Ignition system

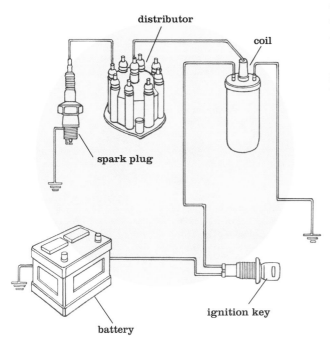

In a traditional ignition system, power passes from the battery to the coil to the distributor and then, in sequential doses, to the spark plugs.

The ignition coil is a small module that sits directly below the distributor cap. In newer cars, this coil can be incorporated into the spark plug wires (sometimes known as ignition cables).

Spark Plugs

You can't see one of your car's spark plugs without removing the spark plug wire and rubber boot (the rubber casing that fits on top of the spark plug) and using a special socket wrench to tug it out. This is a challenging prospect. If the socket wrench isn't positioned properly, the spark plug may break — and removing half of a spark plug from the engine is next to impossible. Your mechanic has the know-how to do it correctly, so make it easy on yourself and just look at the brand-new, still-sparkling spark plug featured on page 54.

At the bottom of the spark plug, a thin metal arm curves under a small bump of metal called the electrode. As high-voltage electricity is forced down the length of the spark plug, it jumps the gap between the arm and the electrode like a miniature bolt of lightning. That "lightning" is the spark that ignites the fuel vapor in the cylinder head.

The size of the gap between the electrode and the lower arm, then, is very important. If the gap is too small or too large, the spark plug won't work efficiently. When mechanics speak of *gapping* a spark plug, they mean that they're adjusting the gap between the electrode and the lower arm to improve the spark plug's performance.

When a spark plug is new, its electrode is square. Under normal driving conditions, the electrode should wear down to a curved shape, and it will acquire carbon deposits. The pattern of wear and carbon deposits on a spark plug can be used as a gauge of the spark plug's firing power. Normal carbon deposits, for example, are light brown or gray. Black carbon deposits can indicate electrical deficiencies. Constant city driving, with lots of stops and starts, often leads to heavy carbon buildup, which shortens the gap and interferes with the spark plug's firing power.

If your engine idles roughly or constantly stalls, it may be a sign that your spark plugs aren't functioning properly. Ask your mechanic to examine the spark plugs. If she finds a problem with them, have them replaced. Even if only one or two of the spark plugs have heavy carbon buildup or uneven electrode wear, replace *all* the spark plugs as well as all the spark plug wires. Why? When all the spark plugs are functioning at the same capacity, electricity flows freely and evenly — and that's what you need for a smooth-running car.

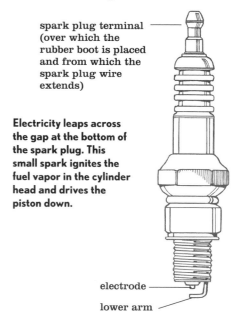

spark plug terminal (over which the rubber boot is placed and from which the spark plug wire extends)

Electricity leaps across the gap at the bottom of the spark plug. This small spark ignites the fuel vapor in the cylinder head and drives the piston down.

electrode

lower arm

The Distributor

The distributor is becoming a thing of the past, but the technology that has replaced it is so new that there are plenty of distributor-carrying cars still on the road. As discussed on page 52, there are three types of ignition systems: breaker-point, breakerless, and distributorless. Only breaker-point and breakerless ignition systems employ distributors. Check your owner's manual or consult with your mechanic to find out which type of ignition system your car has.

If your car has a distributor, you can find it by following the spark plug wires from the engine block. They will lead to a blue or black plastic casing. This is the distributor cap. Underneath it is the actual distributor.

The spark plug wires are joined at the distributor cap by another wire, which feeds electricity to the distributor. The distributor then parcels out the electrical current to the spark plug wires, feeding the spark plugs the electricity they need to fire at the appropriate moment in the piston's cycle.

In newer cars without distributors, the distribution of electricity is controlled by computer.

Finding the distributor

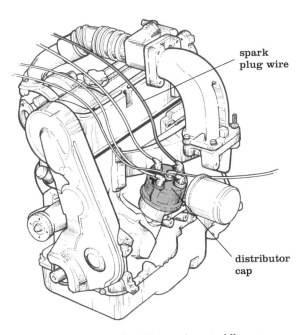

spark
plug wire

distributor
cap

The distributor is located in different places in different cars. To find it, follow the spark plug wires from the engine block; they're connected at the other end to the distributor cap.

The Drivetrain

Okay. So now you have the engine purring and you want to be on your way. The system that liberates power from the engine and uses it to get the wheels turning is called the drivetrain.

The main component of the drivetrain is the transmission. This mass of spinning gears sits close to the engine block. The configuration of the transmission is dependent on your car's drive system, which in most cases will be one of three types: all-wheel drive (AWD), front-wheel drive (FWD), and rear-wheel drive (RWD).

All-wheel drive, also known as four-wheel drive, delivers power equally to all four wheels of the vehicle. The most common AWD vehicles on the road today are sport-utility vehicles (SUVs). SUVs were originally designed for off-road enthusiasts who enjoy driving in rugged terrain. However, statistics — and the view of passing traffic on any North American highway — indicate that a rising population of families are driving SUVs. It's easy to see why — the height and weight of an SUV offer a sense of safety and security when driving, especially with children in the backseat.

Front-wheel drive is the most common drive system on passenger vehicles. For most folks, a FWD car will suffice for traversing the roads between work, home, school, and vacation spots. In a FWD system, the transmission delivers power to the front wheels only; the front wheels pull the car, and the back wheels simply follow them.

Rear-wheel-drive vehicles are the opposite of FWD vehicles; the transmission delivers power to the rear wheels only, and they push the car — and the front wheels — in the right direction.

Shifting Gears

The purpose of the transmission is to transfer appropriate power from the engine to the wheels for different speeds and loads. When you're pulling out into a lane of traffic, for example, you need a lot of power to go from 0 to 30 mph (0 to 50 kph) in a hurry, even though you're not going very fast. If the traffic lane opens out onto a highway, you'll want more speed to get up to 60 mph (100 kph), but you won't need as much power to make the transition.

The load that you're carrying as you stop, start, and speed up affects the power that you need from the transmission.

The transmission is filled with gears of different sizes. In a vehicle with manual transmission, the driver shifts gears to increase or decrease the output of power from the engine. Lower gears deliver high power but aren't capable of great speed; higher gears turn faster but can't deliver as much power as lower gears. The gearshift, or "stick," controls which gears are being used in the transmission. The clutch pedal, when pressed, suspends operation of the transmission while you shift — that is, while you change from one set of gears to another. In a vehicle with automatic transmission, a computer controls the shifting of gears in the transmission.

Manual Transmissions

The gears of a manual transmission are housed in a pan on the underside of the engine. The fluid that lubricates them is called clutch fluid, but it's actually nothing more than brake fluid. That's right — brake fluid is used to engage and disengage the clutch.

The clutch fluid reservoir, called a master cylinder, is usually situated next to the brake fluid master cylinder at the back of the engine. It looks a lot like the brake fluid master cylinder, but it's a little smaller, and its cap is often labeled CLUTCH. As a measure of good preventive maintenance, periodically check the quality and amount of the clutch fluid (see page 6 for details).

Automatic Transmissions

The gears of an automatic transmission are housed in a pan that usually sits in the middle underside of the engine, behind the oil pan. You probably won't be able to see it from the top of the engine, so if you want to take a look at it, ask your mechanic to point it out the next time she has your car up on a hoist.

Red-pink transmission fluid sits inside the pan and starts to move through the drivetrain as soon as you shift into *D* (drive) or *R* (reverse). It keeps the gears lubricated, so that they don't grind against each other. You'll want to check the amount of transmission fluid sitting in the pan (using the handy dipstick) periodically and to top it off, if necessary. See page 62 for details.

The Differential

If you have rear-wheel drive, your drivetrain will extend to the rear of your car. So let's take a look at your rear end — that is, the rear of the drivetrain.

From the transmission, a driveshaft (a long rod) extends along the underside of your car to the rear wheels. At the intersection between the driveshaft and the rear axle (the connecting rod between the two rear wheels) sits the rear differ-ential. The differential is a gearbox filled with bearings, gears, and lubricating fluid. It converts the sideways-spinning motion of the driveshaft into a forward-spinning motion that pulls the rear wheels forward. It also allows the wheels to rotate at different speeds, as needs to happen when your car is making a sharp turn (the wheel on the inside of the turn spins more slowly than the wheel on the outside).

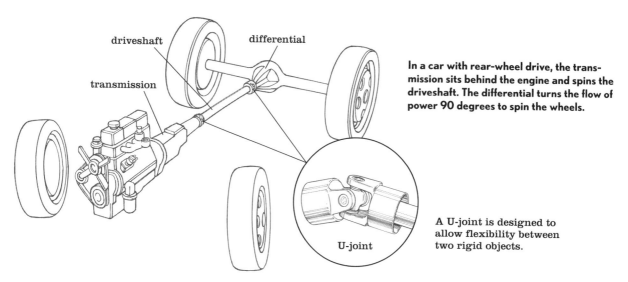

driveshaft

differential

transmission

In a car with rear-wheel drive, the transmission sits behind the engine and spins the driveshaft. The differential turns the flow of power 90 degrees to spin the wheels.

U-joint

A U-joint is designed to allow flexibility between two rigid objects.

The driveshaft is secured by two U-joints (universal joints), which connect it at the rear to the differential and at the front to the transmission. The U-joints allow the driveshaft to bounce around without pulling at the transmission setup.

The Transaxle

If your car has front-wheel drive, the transmission and differential are combined into one unit called the transaxle, which sits beside the engine block. Its purpose is to connect the front wheels to the steering wheel, which, in turn, gives all the power to the front of your car. The joints that connect the axle to the transaxle are called constant velocity joints (CV-joints); they allow maximum flexibility for the axle, so that it can turn the front wheels and bounce freely over bumps in the road.

The transaxle serves as both transmission and front-wheel differential. In a *transverse* engine like this, the transaxle sits beside the engine. In a *longitudinal* engine, the transaxle sits in front of the engine.

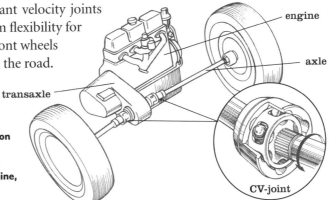

engine

axle

transaxle

CV-joint

A CV-joint allows up-and-down as well as side-to-side movement.

Transmission setups for FWD, RWD, and AWD vehicles

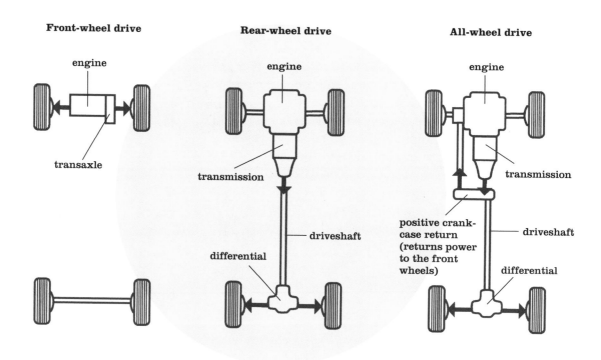

Front-wheel drive

engine

transaxle

Rear-wheel drive

engine

transmission

driveshaft

differential

All-wheel drive

engine

transmission

positive crank-
case return
(returns power
to the front
wheels)

driveshaft

differential

Checking the Clutch Fluid

Checking and topping off the clutch fluid is a task that needs to be done quickly yet carefully. Brake fluid, which is used as clutch fluid, becomes contaminated by exposure to air, so you must work quickly to limit the exposure time. However, you don't want to work so quickly that you splash the fluid everywhere or accidentally brush dirt or other grime into the reservoir.

TOOLS & SUPPLIES

- Clean rag
- Flathead screwdriver
- Clutch fluid (of the type recommended in your owner's manual)

1 Clean the cylinder. Use a rag to wipe down the top of the clutch fluid master cylinder.

2 Remove the cap. Turn the cap counterclockwise or pry it off with a flathead screwdriver.

3 Check the fluid level. Peer inside the master cylinder. The fluid should reach to about ¼ inch (6 mm) below the lip of the reservoir.

➡ If the level of fluid seems fine, simply replace the cap — you're done.

➡ If the level of fluid seems low, pour in brake fluid, being careful not to spill. Then replace the cap.

4 Dispose of the remaining brake fluid. Exposure to air — as limited as it was — has contaminated it, so it's useless to save the leftovers.

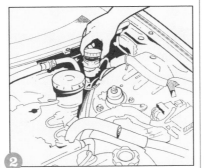

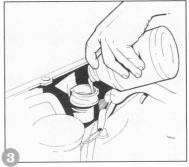

Checking the Automatic Transmission Fluid

Checking and topping off the automatic transmission fluid is a simple procedure. You should rarely have to add automatic transmission fluid. If your transmission fluid pan consistently runs low, have your mechanic evaluate why.

TOOLS & SUPPLIES

- Clean rag
- Funnel
- 1 quart (liter) automatic transmission fluid (of the type recommended in your owner's manual)

1 **Park your car on level ground.** Set the parking brake and leave the engine idling. (This is one of the very few maintenance tasks for which you should leave the engine idling.)

2 **Locate the transmission fluid dipstick.** It usually sits just behind or in front of the engine block. Its cap is often yellow or red and may be labeled TRANS FLUID. Pull it out and wipe it clean with a rag.

3 **Take a look at the end of the clean dipstick.** Some dipsticks have two grooves, one marked FULL or F and the other EMPTY or E. Others have separate COLD and HOT grids, as shown in the illustration.

4 **Reinsert the dipstick.** Push the dipstick into the hole from which you just removed it, as far as it will go. Then pull it out.

5 **Check the fluid level.** Take note of how high up the dipstick the transmission fluid reaches. The fluid should reach the FULL mark or be within the HOT grid. It should *not* be below or above the mark or grid.

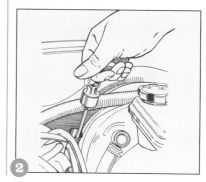

6 **Check the fluid quality.**
Touch the liquid on the dipstick.
It should feel warm, not hot.
How does it look? Automatic
transmission fluid should be red-
dish in color. Bubbles in the fluid
may signal that the fluid is old
and needs to be replaced. Smell
the fluid. A burnt smell means
that the automatic transmission
gears are burning out and should
be evaluated by your mechanic.

➡ **If the level and quality of
the automatic transmission
fluid seems fine,** replace the dipstick — you're done.

➡ **If the level of the transmission fluid is less than it should
be,** insert the skinny end of a
funnel into the hole from which
you removed the dipstick.

7 **Add transmission fluid.** Add
the fluid slowly, stopping to use

the dipstick to check the level of
fluid in the pan. Stop adding
fluid when the dipstick tells you
that the pan is full.

8 **Reinsert the dipstick and
push it down tight,** so that the
handle seals the hole.

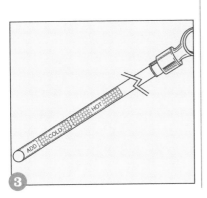

TOPPING OFF

As a rule of thumb, the
amount of fluid that it
would take to move the fill
level of the transmission
fluid pan from the EMPTY
groove to the FULL groove
on the dipstick equals about
½ quart (0.5 L). Using this
as a guide, you can deduce
about how much fluid you
need to add.

The Cooling System

The cooling system is miraculously multi-functional and essential to the health of your car's engine. However, much of it is hidden from sight, so now's a good time to take a break from your under-the-hood inspection and cool off yourself. Grab a drink, sit on the back steps, and take a literary walk through the cooling system.

The radiator is a long, thin metal grid that sits upright at the front of the engine. It's filled with coolant (an antifreeze-water mixture). Coolant flows from the radiator through the lower radiator hose to the engine block. Inside the engine, it runs through passages built into the cylinders and absorbs some of the heat that they exude. The heated coolant then takes a short detour by way of the heater core, which can allow some of the heat to pass into the passenger compartment. Eventually the coolant flows from the upper engine block, past the thermostat, and through the upper radiator hose back to the radiator.

The forward movement of your car, assisted by a fan located behind the radiator core, allows air to flow over the radiator, cooling the coolant. The water pump drives coolant through the system in a never-ending cycle, sensors monitor the coolant's temperature, and a recovery tank houses excess coolant.

That may sound complicated, but really it's fairly simple, and it boils down to three things: The cooling system absorbs heat from the engine to keep it running efficiently. It helps lubricate engine components. And as a happy by-product, it warms you and all the other the occupants inside your car when the temperatures become chilly.

Coolant

The liquid coolant that circulates through the cooling system is a mixture of antifreeze and water. Sometimes this antifreeze-water mixture is called simply *antifreeze*. For the sake of clarity, we'll continue to use the term *coolant* — we don't want to confuse pure bottled antifreeze with the diluted stuff that you use in your car. If you filled your car's cooling system with pure antifreeze, it would soon gel into a sludgelike mixture. Your mechanic would then have to flush the entire cooling system to clean it, while you stood by wringing your hands and hoping that no expensive damage resulted.

The Radiator

Now let's get back to our under-the-hood survey. At the very front of the engine compartment, sometimes partially hidden under the lip of the car frame, is the radiator. It looks like a very sturdy mesh grid with a solid metal top. A small cap is set on the top. (If you see a smaller radiator-like grid set in front of the actual radiator, that's the air-conditioning condenser.)

The radiator should be black or gray in color; any greenish discoloration indicates a coolant leak. Its front should be free from debris; if it is caked with dead bugs or leaves, you can spray-wash it. (Be sure the engine is cold when you do so — spraying cold water on a hot radiator could cause it to burst.)

When the cooling system warms up, it becomes pressurized — that is, the coolant starts circulating under extremely high pressure. The radiator cap is designed to seal the cooling system,

The cooling system

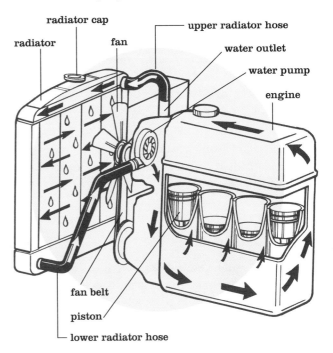

Seen from behind and isolated from the rest of the engine, the cooling system becomes simply a circuitous routing of coolant through the engine.

preventing the system from leaking when the engine is hot. *Never* remove the radiator cap while the engine is hot; the hot, pressurized coolant could burst out, causing serious burns to your hands and face. Even when you are sure that the engine is cool, take precautions when removing the radiator cap. Wear gloves. Stand away from the radiator, so that your head is not directly over it. Press a rag against the near side of the cap to stop any coolant from splashing on you. As you open the cap, tilt it so that the opening points away from you.

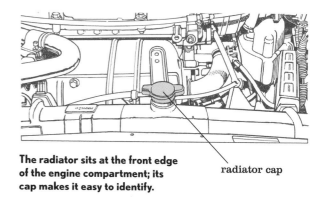

The radiator sits at the front edge of the engine compartment; its cap makes it easy to identify.

radiator cap

CAUTION

Never touch the radiator when the engine is warm, or even lukewarm. Always wait until the engine is completely cool before removing the radiator cap or tinkering with the radiator or any other part of the cooling system. But don't let the cooling system scare you — when the engine is cool, it's perfectly safe.

Tilt the cap away from you as you open it, so that if there is a sudden release of pressure from the cooling system — which could happen *only* if the engine hasn't been allowed to cool down — rising coolant won't splash onto you.

Radiator Hoses

Extending from either side of the radiator core is a hose — the upper radiator hose is on one side and the lower radiator hose on the other. The upper radiator hose, naturally, sits higher on the radiator than the lower radiator hose. It draws hot coolant from the engine block into the radiator, where it is cooled. If you follow the upper radiator hose from the radiator, it'll take you to the engine block.

The lower radiator hose directs coolant to the water pump, and from there it is passed into the engine block. It circulates through the engine block and then returns to the radiator by way of the upper radiator hose.

Before you turn your attention away from the lower radiator hose, take a good look around it to see if you can spot the drain plug at the bottom of the radiator. The drain plug, referred to as the petcock, extends slightly from the radiator and has a tap-type attachment on its end. When the cooling system needs to be flushed — check your owner's manual to find out how often this needs to happen — your mechanic will open the tap on the petcock to drain coolant from the cooling system.

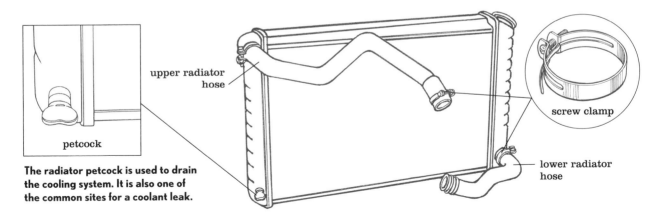

petcock

The radiator petcock is used to drain the cooling system. It is also one of the common sites for a coolant leak.

upper radiator hose

screw clamp

lower radiator hose

Because the engine is cold, it's okay to touch the radiator hoses. Place a bit of pressure on each one. Both hoses should feel firm; gently pinching each hose should not bring its two sides together. Take a look as well at the clamps that secure the hoses to the radiator. These clamps are called screw clamps because you need a flathead screwdriver to loosen and tighten them (see the illustration on page 67).

The radiator cap reminds do-it-yourselfers to wait until the engine is cool before unsealing the radiator.

Coolant Recovery Tank

Most vehicles today have a coolant recovery tank (also referred to as an antifreeze recovery tank) located to one side of the engine. It's a see-through plastic container that contains green or orange fluid (that's the coolant). A small hose extends from the top of the radiator to the recovery tank, and another small hose hangs from the the recovery tank and leads nowhere. What's the purpose of the two hoses? When coolant heats up, it expands, creating more coolant than your cooling system can hold. The excess coolant flows through the small hose extending from the radiator to the coolant recovery tank. When the system cools off and the coolant contracts, the decreased pressure in the radiator draws back coolant from the recovery tank. In the event that the recovery tank is overfilled, it leaks coolant through the small hose that isn't attached to anything on its other end. This can make a huge mess under the hood, with coolant splashing all over the engine. But it's safer than having an airtight cooling system that, when placed under too much pressure from expanding coolant, could explode.

A quick check to ensure that there is an appropriate amount — not too much and not too little — of coolant in the cooling system is to compare the level of coolant in the coolant recovery tank to the "max" or "hot" and "min" or "cold" marks on the outside of the tank wall. Because you are looking at a cold engine (right?), the amount of coolant should be at or near the bottom mark ("min" or "cold"). If there is insufficient coolant in the reservoir, read the next section before turning to Checking the Coolant on page 70.

Temperature Sensors

Two sensors monitor the temperature of the coolant; one sits in the radiator and the other in the engine block. When you first start your car, the coolant is cold — that is, at the ambient temperature — and the needle in your dashboard temperature gauge sits at the bottom of the gauge. As your car warms up and the cooling system kicks into action, the coolant begins to warm up. The sensors transmit this information to the temperature gauge, and the arrow should slowly rise from the bottom (cold) to the middle (just right). If the arrow enters the upper red zone (too hot), it could indicate that your engine is overheating. Of course, it also may mean that the temperature sensors have malfunctioned. (Turn to page 210 for advice on what to do when the temperature gauge needle jumps into the hot zone.)

Checking the Coolant

Keep in mind that the cooling system is designed to be a tightly sealed operation. You shouldn't have to add more coolant to it. If your coolant level frequently runs low, start looking good and hard for a coolant leak.

Be sure that the engine is cold when you perform this maintenance check.

TOOLS & SUPPLIES

- Rubber gloves
- Antifreeze
- Plastic bowl or container
- Water (tap water is fine)
- Antifreeze tester (available at most auto parts stores)
- Funnel
- Clean rag

1 Examine the coolant recovery tank. The level of liquid it contains should rise to the "min" or "cold" mark on the tank's outer wall.

2 Open the radiator cap. Wear rubber gloves and follow the precautions given on page 66.

3 Check the fluid level in the radiator. The coolant should rise to about 2 inches (5 cm) from the top of the radiator.

➡ **If the level of coolant in both the recovery tank and the radiator seems fine,** replace the radiator cap and congratulate yourself for a job well done.

➡ **If the level of coolant seems fine in the tank but low in the radiator, or vice versa,** the small overflow hose that connects the tank and the radiator may be clogged, preventing coolant from flowing between them. If that's the case, replace the cap, then give your mechanic a ring and ask her for an appointment. She may have to disconnect the hose and clean it.

➡ **If the level of coolant in both the tank and the radiator seems low,** replace the radiator cap and grab the rest of your

supplies. You'll need to mix up a batch of coolant and add it to the system, as described in the following steps.

4 **Prepare a batch of coolant.** Pour a bit of antifreeze into a medium-size plastic bowl or container. Pour an equal measure of water into it.

5 **Test the coolant.** Dip the end of the antifreeze tester into the antifreeze-water mixture. Then remove the tester and read it. The liquid should have a strength of -32°F (0°C).

6 **Adjust the coolant strength as necessary.** If the coolant strength is not quite down to -32°F (0°C), add a splash of antifreeze to the bowl. If it's below -32°F (0°C), add a splash of water. Test the coolant again, and keep mixing and testing until the coolant has reached the right strength.

7 **Identify the coolant refill location.** In most cars, coolant is added to the cooling system through the coolant recovery tank. In some cars, however, it's added to the radiator. Check your owner's manual to find out which is the case with your car.

8 **Top off the coolant.** Remove the cap from the coolant recovery tank. Stick the skinny end of the funnel into the tank and carefully pour the antifreeze-water mixture through the funnel into the tank. Watch the level of coolant in the tank care-fully; it should rise just to the level of — not above — that "min" or "cold" mark.

9 **Clean up.** When the tank is full, replace its cap. Use a clean rag to wipe down the exterior of the tank.

Dispose of any leftover pre-mixed coolant. Store the anti-freeze in a safe location, where children and pets won't be able to get into it.

Fan

When your car is moving, air rushes in over the radiator, helping cool the coolant. The fan, which sits just behind the radiator, is the mechanical companion to this naturally inspired phenomenon. The fan blows air onto the radiator from behind. If you're stuck in traffic and your car is idling, idling, idling, the fan is the only cooling influence on the radiator.

The fan is usually attached at its back end to the water pump, which we'll discuss next. In older cars, the fan is driven by a belt called, aptly, the fan belt; if your car has one, you'll see it wrapped around the base of the fan. Check the fan belt periodically; it should be snug, meaning that it gives no more than ½ inch (1 cm) when you press on it, but not too tight, and it shouldn't have cracks or fraying edges.

Newer cars have an electric fan that is driven by a motor and regulated by a temperature switch. Be cautious in your work under the hood if this is the type of fan in your car, because the fan can kick on any time the engine is hot — even if it is not running. Be absolutely sure the engine is cool before you get your hands anywhere near this fan.

Water Pump

The water pump pulls coolant from the radiator through the lower radiator hose and circulates it through the cooling system. To find the pump, just follow the path of the lower radiator hose.

An easy way to check whether the water pump is working at maximum power is to place both hands on the fan blades (it's okay, the engine is cold, so nothing is going to start moving unexpectedly) and gently rock them. If there is excessive movement, the water pump is likely not working at full efficiency. The looseness could also be a symptom of a worn bearing or gasket. Enlist the expertise of your mechanic to figure out how to fix the problem.

Thermostat

This little unit allows the engine to warm up as quickly as possible, thereby improving engine efficiency and economizing on fuel. The thermostat is a heat-sensitive valve located just outside the engine block. You won't be able to see it, but if you follow the upper radiator hose, you'll find that it connects to a small metal housing unit (called the water outlet) attached to the engine block. The thermostat sits inside the water outlet.

When the engine is cold — as it is when you first start up your car — the thermostat valve stays closed, preventing coolant from flowing. The coolant that is trapped near the engine block begins to heat up as the cylinders fire, in turn helping the engine heat up quickly. As the coolant warms, the thermostat valve slowly opens, allowing the coolant to begin to pass through to the radiator. When the engine is hot, the thermostat valve opens fully, and the cooling system operates at full throttle.

So you see, the cooling system is not just a cooling system; it's also an engine-heating system that brings your car to optimal fuel-conversion efficiency as fast as possible. Nifty, isn't it?

Occasionally a thermostat will become sticky, meaning that it doesn't open and close as it should. Heating and cooling problems result. If you find that the passenger compartment in your car doesn't warm up properly or that your engine tends to overheat, ask your mechanic to take a look at the thermostat for possible defects.

A COOLING SYSTEM CHECKUP

Check	Look For
Coolant	Should rise to about 2 inches (5 cm) below the top of the radiator and to the "cold" or "min" mark in the recovery tank. If there's less than that, you need to add more coolant.
Fan belt (if you have one)	Should give no more than ½ inch (1 cm) when you press on it. Check for frays and cracks.
Radiator hoses	Should be flexible and firm, with no cracks. Check the ends for signs of a coolant leak.
Radiator core	Examine the outside of the radiator for spots of green — this could signal a coolant leak. Wash away any debris that may be obstructing the front exterior of the radiator.

Heater Core

You might not think that the heating system has much to do with the cooling system, but, in fact, they are one and the same. It's amazingly simple.

The coolant runs throughout the engine block and gets hot. Before it starts moving back to the radiator to get cooled off, the coolant takes a detour of sorts through a miniature radiator called the heater core. The heater core absorbs some of the heat from the coolant and becomes hot itself. When your toes are cold and you want to warm them up, you flip the heater switch inside your car. The switch starts up a blower motor (or electrical fan) that blows air across the heater core, where it's warmed up, and into ventilation outlets that distribute the warm air in the interior of your car.

Air-Conditioning

If your car has air-conditioning, you can look at the system, but don't touch. The a/c system is highly pressurized, and no one but a trained professional should fiddle with it. Instead, follow the path of components in the diagram on page 75, and see if you can find them in your own engine.

Heating system

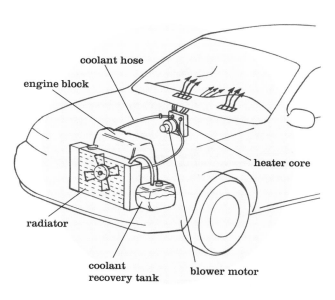

coolant hose

engine block

heater core

radiator

coolant recovery tank

blower motor

Hot coolant makes a loop through the back of the engine, passing close to the firewall that separates the interior of the car from the engine. If you turn on the heat in your car, a blower motor starts up, blowing air over the hot coolant to push that heat into the passenger compartment.

Air-conditioning system

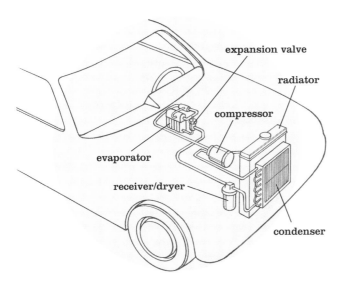

expansion valve

radiator

compressor

evaporator

receiver/dryer

condenser

The air-conditioning system sucks heat out of the air that passes into the interior of your car. It's an extremely high-pressure system, and refrigerant is definitely not something you want to inhale or touch, so this is one bit of under-the-hood maintenance that you should leave to a professional. You can look, but don't touch.

Refrigerant is interesting stuff. Why? It's easy to compress and it has a very low boiling point. That's what makes it useful for cooling the air inside your car. Here's how it works.

The evaporator sits at the back of the engine compartment. It's a heat exchanger; it allows cold refrigerant to absorb heat from the surrounding air. Because refrigerant has such a low boiling point, that bit of heat causes it to boil, transforming it into a gas. (And according to the laws of physics, as it changes from a liquid to a gaseous state, it can absorb even more heat.)

How does refrigerant get cold? It's actually a very straightforward process. From the evaporator, the high-temperature gaseous refrigerant passes to the compressor, where it is compressed into a high-pressure, high-temperature gas. From there it is passed to the condensor, a radiator-like device that sits in front of the actual radiator and works like the actual radiator. As air flowing in from the front of your car and being pushed by the fan behind the radiator passes over the condensor, it cools the refrigerant, returning it to its liquid state.

The receiver/dryer accepts the high-pressure, low-temperature liquid refrigerant from the condensor and holds it. It sorts out any remaining gas-state refrigerant so that only liquid passes on from this point. The receiver/dryer then gives the liquid refrigerant to the expansion valve, which sits just outside the evaporator and regulates how much refrigerant passes into it.

Inside the evaporator, the now low-pressure, low-temperature refrigerant begins to absorb heat from outside air again. A blower motor sits outside the evaporator and blows air across it. The refrigerant inside the evaporator absorbs heat from the passing air, cooling it. The cooled air then passes into the interior of your car, making it a more comfortable environment for you and your passengers during hot, swampy weather.

The refrigerant in the air-conditioning system in your car is either the environmentally friendly CFC-free refrigerant R-134a or the old R-12 refrigerant known as Freon. When researchers discovered that Freon contributes to the breakdown of the ozone layer, Freon stopped being the refrigerant of choice for air conditioners. In fact,

as of 1995, all manufacturing of Freon ceased. In the event that your Freon-based air-conditioning system requires more refrigerant, you can still find existing stock of Freon, but it's expensive. You cannot add R-134a refrigerant to a system that requires Freon. You can upgrade your system to use a CFC-free refrigerant, though. Ask your mechanic for advice. It might be more economically advantageous for you to make do without air-conditioning.

AUTOTALK

Switch on the air conditioner for a few minutes every week, even when it's cold outside and you'd rather have heat. Why? Doing so circulates the refrigerant inside the hoses, keeping them and the rubber seals around them from drying out.

Engine Oil

Engine oil is the lifeblood of your engine. It lubricates engine parts, allowing them to work efficiently, and, by cutting down on friction, helps keep the engine cool. Without adequate oil, or with thick and dirty oil, engine components grind against each other. They heat up and wear down quickly. Worn-out parts, it stands to reason, cannot do what they are supposed to do, which ultimately means more engine problems and higher repair bills.

Changing the oil regularly is the number-one best way to prolong the life and efficiency of your engine. You should have the oil changed every 3,000 miles (5,000 km) or every 3 months; check your owner's manual for specific recommendations.

What You Can't See

You can't see much of the oil lubrication system from under the hood. When it's not circulating through the engine, oil is held in the oil pan. The pan sits below the crankshaft, at the bottom of the engine block. The oil pump, which is located near or even inside the oil pan, moves oil from the oil pan to the engine and then back to the pan. On its route to the engine, the oil passes through an oil filter, a round metal cylinder containing pleated sheets of paper set together tightly to strain impurities from the engine oil.

The oil filter should be replaced every time the oil is changed; your mechanic will do this as a matter of course. Oil pumps, on the other hand, are built to last, so you shouldn't ever have to worry about yours — that is, unless you don't change your oil and filter regularly. Dirty oil can muck up the valve inside the pump, causing it to stick. When the oil pump doesn't work, it must be replaced; it cannot be repaired.

What You Can See

The components of the oil lubrication system that you can see under the hood — the oil fill-hole cap and the oil dipstick — are the only parts that you really need to be familiar with.

The oil fill-hole allows you to feed your engine more oil. Look for a round cap (sometimes marked "engine oil") somewhere on the top of the engine block. Unscrew the cap by turning it counterclockwise. The cap should have a rubber ring around its inside; this seals the fill-hole and keeps contaminants from getting in. If it looks dirty, get a clean rag and wipe it clean.

Take a peek down into the fill-hole. Now you're looking at the inside of the engine block. When oil is poured into this hole, it makes its way through the cylinder heads (where the pistons sit) and down through the crankcase and crankshaft to eventually reach the oil pan.

Put the fill-hole cap back on and take a look around for the engine oil dipstick. It has a curved handle (sometimes it's yellow) and might say "engine oil" or "oil" on it. Can't find it? Consult your owner's manual, which will indicate its loca-tion. The dipstick is nothing more than a long, thin strip of metal. It's long for a reason — it must reach all the way down into the oil pan so that you can find out how much engine oil is in the pan. To get a reading, you simply wipe the dipstick clean, push it all the way into its tube, then pull it out and examine how much oil its end is coated with. The oil coating corresponds to the depth of oil in the pan. Pages 82–83 offer more detail.

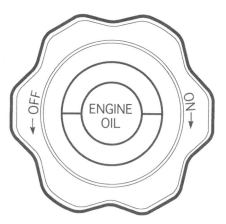

The fill-hole cap is usually located on top of the engine block. It will read ENGINE OIL loud and clear.

Choosing the Right Engine Oil

The first step in choosing the right oil for your car is to check your owner's manual; it will tell you which type of oil is recommended for your car. (Jot down this information on the Vehicle Specifications Record on page 239.)

So, just what do all those letters and numbers on engine oil labels really mean? Oil's ability to flow — in other words, its thickness — is called viscosity. When the engine is cold, it stands to reason that the engine oil is also cold and more viscous. As the engine warms up, so does the engine oil, and it becomes less viscous. Its initial viscosity determines how easily it starts moving throughout the engine.

This means that in cold temperatures, you probably should use a thinner oil that can move quickly through the engine. In warm temperatures, you'd want a thicker oil that would be able to maintain some viscosity. For convenience, most oils are multigrade — they can handle both situations.

SAE 5W30 and SAE 10W30 are the two most common types of oil for passenger cars. The two sets of numbers (separated by a "W") let you know

AUTOTALK

If you have a car with an automatic transmission, don't confuse the oil dipstick with the transmission fluid dipstick. Examine both carefully to determine which is which. Some oil dipsticks have "engine oil" written on them. Some transmission fluid dipsticks have "trans fluid" written on them. The hole that the transmission fluid dipstick reaches into is relatively large, as this is also the hole into which you pour transmission fluid. The hole that the oil dipstick reaches into is smaller, because it is not the hole into which you pour engine oil; there's a separate fill-hole for that.

Engine oil label

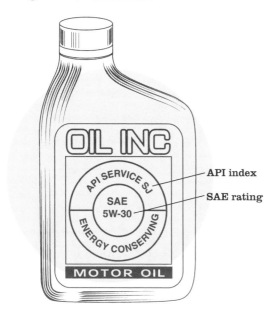

API index

SAE rating

The label on a bottle of engine oil will give both its SAE rating and its API index. Check your owner's manual to find out what type is recommended for your vehicle.

that they are multigrade oils, suitable for cold and warm temperatures. The lower the first number, the thinner the oil is, and, hence, the better it works during the winter months. The higher the second number, the better able the oil is to maintain viscosity at high temperatures. Contrary to popular opinion, the "W" in these labels stands for "winter," not "weight." SAE is the acronym for the Society of Automotive Engineers, which came up with this grading system.

5W30 engine oil, for example, is better suited for very cold temperatures than is 10W30. The two will have the same effectiveness in warmer temperatures.

Always use the grade of oil recommended by your car's manufacturer, even when you're just topping off. In other words, if your owner's manual states that the recommended oil grade is 5W30, use 5W30 oil, not 10W30 or 5W40. The engine will run best when you feed it the oil it's designed to use. It's a good idea to keep a bottle of the right type of oil in your automotive tool kit (see page 189). This way, you're always assured of having the right kind of oil at hand when you need it.

Oil is also classified in a system developed by the American Petroleum Institute (API). The API index is based on the performance value of the oil, which, in turn, is based on the additives — those that control rust, improve fuel economy, control deposits, and so on — in the oil.

The API index is represented on a bottle of oil by two letters. For passenger cars and light trucks, the first letter is always an *S*. (Never buy oil that has an API rating beginning with a *C*; that's for commercial applications.) The second letter indicates the span of years in which that particular type of oil was introduced. The letters have progressed as the years have worn on since the introduction of the API system. The first classification, for example, launched back in 1952, was SA. Now we're up to SL.

If your car is not a recent make and model, your owner's manual might recommend an oil with an SE, SF, SG, SH, or SJ rating. You can always use oil that has a newer rating (further down the alphabet) than that recommended for your car. It will simply exceed the standards set by the manufacturer of your car.

AUTOTALK

Earlier (page 63), you learned that it takes ½ quart (0.5 L) of automatic transmission fluid to increase the level of fluid in the transmission fluid pan from the "empty" to the "full" groove on the dipstick. A similar guideline applies to engine oil and the engine oil dipstick. In this case, however, the grooves on the dipstick are farther apart, and the distance between them amounts to about 1 quart (1 L) of oil.

Checking the Oil

The easiest way to check the quality and quantity of engine oil is to use the oil dipstick. For this two-minute task, all you need is a clean rag. If it turns out that you need to top off the engine oil, just reach into the automotive tool kit you keep in your trunk (see page 189) and pull out a funnel and a bottle of engine oil.

TOOLS & SUPPLIES

- Clean rag
- Funnel
- Engine oil (of the type recommended in your owner's manual)

① Park your car on level ground. If you've been driving, let your car sit for a few minutes before checking the oil. This will allow the engine oil to settle back into the oil pan so that you can get a more accurate reading.

② Remove the oil dipstick. Its end, which reaches into the oil pan, will be coated with engine oil. Wipe it clean with a rag.

③ Examine the stick carefully. It will have two marks on its lower end; on the lower end you'll see *L* (for "low") or *E* (for "empty"), and just above you'll see *H* (for "high") or *F* (for "full").

④ Insert the dipstick into the hole from which you just drew it. Push it all the way back in, then slowly pull it out.

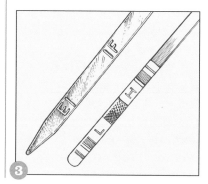

⑤ Examine the oil. Oil from the pan should coat the stick to a point about three-quarters of the way from the *L* mark to the *H* mark. If it doesn't, you'll need to add more oil. Examine the quality of the oil as well. It should be light brown in color; if it's any darker than that, it's time to have your mechanic change the oil.

➡ **If the oil seems fine,** you're done — just replace the dipstick.

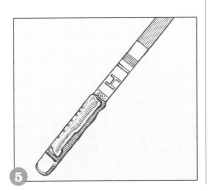

➡ **If you need to add more oil,** move on to the next step.

⑥ Remove the cap of the oil fill-hole. The fill-hole cap is usually located at the top of the engine block. Remove the cap by turning it counterclockwise.

⑦ Add oil. Put the skinny end of the funnel into the fill-hole. Pour in enough oil to fill the oil pan, periodically stopping to check the amount of oil in the pan by using the dipstick. Do not overfill the pan.

⑧ Clean up. Remove the funnel. Wipe around the edge of the fill-hole with a rag, then screw the cap back on. Wipe the funnel with the rag and put it and the bottle of oil in your supplies box.

READING THE OIL

Appearance	What It Means
Light brown or honey	The oil is fresh and clean.
Black	The oil is dirty and needs to be changed.
Reddish	Automatic transmission fluid is leaking into the oil pan. Ask your mechanic to check for a leak.
Milky	Coolant may be seeping into your oil pan. Ask your mechanic to check for a leak.
Water bubbles appear in the oil	Coolant may be seeping into your oil pan, or your engine oil is very, very dirty. Have the oil changed, and if that doesn't fix the problem, ask your mechanic to check for a coolant leak.

Belts and Hoses

Belts and hoses are intertwined throughout the engine. Each has a function, and sometimes multiple functions. When you're peering over, under, and sideways at the engine trying to pin down the cause of a mechanical problem, don't overlook the belts and hoses. They get a lot of action, and they certainly don't last forever. Belts snap. Hoses leak or burst. Thankfully, they are generally much less expensive to replace than the engine parts that they service.

Belt Power

Belts help transfer power. The air conditioner, alternator, camshaft, crankshaft, power steering pump, water pump — all are run by belts. Belts can be the old-style V-belt or the newer, longer-lasting serpentine belt.

Regardless of which type they are, belts should be neither so tight that they're under strain nor so loose that they can't do their job effectively. In addition, being too tight or too loose can lead to a belt snapping. If a belt does break, you'll probably have to have your car towed to your mechanic for repair. A new belt will stretch, so bring your car back to your mechanic after you've driven it around for a couple of weeks to have the belt retightened.

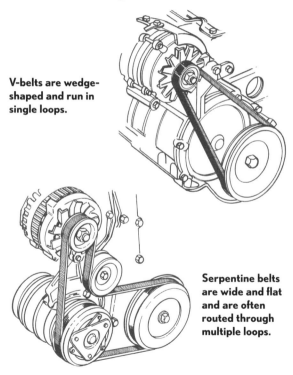

V-belts are wedge-shaped and run in single loops.

Serpentine belts are wide and flat and are often routed through multiple loops.

Some vehicles have a timing belt (or chain). The timing belt drives the crankshaft. (That's a part of the engine block, remember? See page 32.) However, you can't monitor the condition of the timing belt because it's usually covered with a plastic shield that guards it against air and dirt. Check your owner's manual for the mileage at which it's recommended that you replace the timing belt, and follow through on that recommendation. Replacing the timing belt is costly, but it won't be nearly as expensive as replacing the engine parts that will be damaged should the timing belt snap.

Hose Connections

Hoses carry fluids from one part of your car to another. There are plenty of them: radiator hoses, refrigerant hoses, bypass hoses, fuel-injection-system hoses, heater hoses, and more. They're usually color-coded or categorized by size. The clamps that hold them in place can also identify them. For example, as we discussed earlier, the two radiator hoses are held in place by screw clamps. Spring clamps or wire clamps are usually used on fuel lines.

Faulty or old hoses will eventually burst. With a quick examination every month or so, you can prevent this from happening. Inspect the hoses for wear and tear, such as cracks at their ends (where the clamps are). Feel the hoses, applying just a gentle pressure; they should be firm and round. If a hose is flat or has cracks, have it and the clamps that secure it replaced.

Never tinker with the hoses in the air-conditioning unit or fuel-injection system, as they are under high pressure. Examine them closely, but do not pull at or press down hard upon them. Always leave the repair of these hoses to your mechanic.

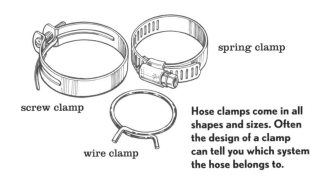

screw clamp

spring clamp

wire clamp

Hose clamps come in all shapes and sizes. Often the design of a clamp can tell you which system the hose belongs to.

Fluid Reservoirs

Keeping vital fluids at the appropriate levels is one of the easiest maintenance measures, and it will greatly reduce the occurrence of costly engine repairs. It doesn't take much time, either.

Automatic Transmission Fluid

If your car has an automatic transmission, it also has automatic transmission fluid, which you should check periodically for quality and quantity. It's easy enough to do. Simply park your car on level ground, leave the engine idling, and use the transmission fluid dipstick to check the level of fluid in your system. See page 62 for complete instructions.

Brake Fluid

Brake fluid is held in the brake master cylinder, which is located near the back of the engine, under the windshield. For operational efficiency, the brakes need good-quality brake fluid. See page 89 for advice on checking and topping off the brake fluid.

Clutch Fluid

If your car is a standard — that is, it has a manual transmission — you'll want to periodically check the amount and quality of clutch fluid. The clutch fluid is housed in a master cylinder near the back of the engine, under the windshield. It often sits close to the brake master cylinder. See page 61 for more information.

Coolant

Coolant, as we discussed earlier, is a mixture of antifreeze and water that circulates through the cooling system, carrying heat away from the engine

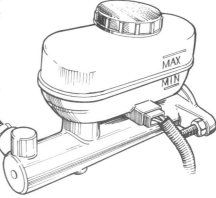

The brake fluid master cylinder is located at the back of the engine. Brake fluid flows from this reservoir through the brake lines to the brakes.

block. If you run low on coolant, your engine is in danger of overheating. But it's quite easy to check the coolant level. See page 70 for details.

Power Steering Fluid

Power steering is a system of hydraulics that makes it easier to turn the steering wheel. If you've ever driven an older car without power steering, you'll appreciate the ease that power steering brings to your driving experience, and you'll have good motivation to make sure that your car is always supplied with adequate power steering fluid.

Power steering fluid is usually good for the life of your car, but it's wise to check it periodically. See page 90 for more information.

Windshield Washer Fluid

Windshield washer fluid keeps the windshield free of bugs, dust, grime, snow, ice, and other viewing obstacles. It's important to check the washer fluid reservoir every week to make sure you have enough fluid, because a dry washer fluid tank can turn your regular commute into hazardous duty. See page 96 for details.

AUTOTALK

Many fluid reservoirs have a dipstick that reaches down into them. Dipsticks make it easy to check the amount of fluid in a reservoir that is hard to reach. You simply pull out the dipstick, wipe it clean, reinsert it, then pull it out and take a reading. The only "tool" you need is a clean rag. Why can't you take a reading right when you first pull out the dipstick? As you've been driving the car around, fluid has been sloshing around in the reservoir pan, perhaps coating more of the dipstick than it rightfully should. You must wipe the dipstick clean and then reinsert it into a placid pan in order to get an accurate reading.

Under-the-hood caps

Engine oil

Radiator

Brake fluid

Power steering fluid

Automatic
transmission fluid

Windshield
wiper fluid

Clutch fluid

Checking the Brake Fluid

Working with brake fluid can be tricky. Brakes don't function well if air, moisture, or dirt gets into the brake lines, because these outside elements can eat into the hoses. Then the brake lines must be bled out — a repair your checkbook won't be happy to accommodate. So when you check the amount and quality of brake fluid in the master cylinder, work fast and work clean!

TOOLS & SUPPLIES

- Clean rag
- Flathead screwdriver (if the master cylinder cap needs to be pried off)
- Brake fluid (of the type recommended in your owner's manual)

1 Find the brake fluid master cylinder. It's recognizable by its cap (see page 88).

2 Examine the fluid. Wipe clean the top of the master cylinder with a rag. Then open the cap. (Some brake master cylinders are transparent, so you don't have to remove the cap to check the level of fluid.) The fluid should rise to about ¼ inch (6 mm) from the top of the reservoir.

Check the quality of the fluid by dipping a finger in it. Rub the liquid between your fingers. If it feels gritty, you'll want to have the fluid changed.

➡ **If the brake fluid seems fine,** replace the cap — you're done!

➡ **If the brake fluid level is low,** you'll have to add more.

3 Top off the fluid. Slowly pour brake fluid into the reservoir. Dumping in fluid as if you were intending to imitate a thunderous waterfall can encourage water droplets to accumulate in the cylinder, leading to rust and braking difficulties. Stop when the brake fluid level rises to about ¼ inch (6 mm) from the top of the reservoir.

4 Replace the cap. Use a clean rag to wipe the inside of the cap, and then set it back on the master cylinder.

5 Dispose of leftovers. Even if you haven't used up all the fluid in the bottle, dispose of it. A half-full container of brake fluid quickly absorbs contaminants from the air, rendering it useless.

Checking the Power Steering Fluid

Some power steering fluid reservoirs are transparent. If that's the case in your car, peer inside to make sure the container is full — the liquid should rise to about 2 inches (5 cm) from the top — and that the fluid is clear or yellow in color.

If your car's power steering fluid reservoir is not transparent, you'll have to open it and use the dipstick, following the steps at right.

1 **Locate the power steering fluid reservoir.** It's usually situated near the front of the engine. Like most reservoir caps, the power steering fluid reservoir cap is labeled, to help you figure out what's what under the hood. (If you can't find it, consult your owner's manual, which will indicate its location.)

2 **Remove the power steering fluid reservoir cap.** You'll find that the dipstick is mounted beneath the cap. Wipe the dipstick clean with a rag.

3 **Examine the clean dipstick.** There will be two grooves on the dipstick. The mark on the far end of the dipstick indicates the level of fluid that should be in

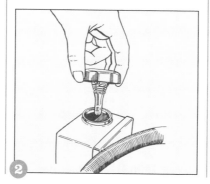

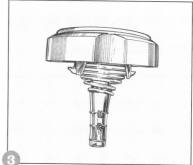

the pan when the engine is cool. The mark closer to the cap indicates the level of fluid that should be in the pan when the engine is warm.

④ **Check the fluid.** Reinsert the dipstick, pushing it in as far as it will go. Then pull it back out. Examine the dipstick; the fluid should rise to the appropriate mark, and the fluid should be clear or yellow.

➡ **If everything looks good,** reinsert the dipstick — you're done!

➡ **If the fluid is not clear or yellow,** bring the car to your mechanic for an evaluation.

➡ **If the level of fluid looks low,** you'll need to add some.

⑤ **Top off the fluid.** Stick the skinny end of the funnel into the hole from which you just drew the dipstick. That's the power steering fluid fill-hole. Carefully pour in power steering fluid, periodically stopping to check the amount of fluid in the reservoir by using the dipstick. Take care not to overfill the reservoir.

⑥ **Replace the cap.** When the level of fluid is appropriate, put the cap back on.

⑦ **Store the leftover power steering fluid.** Cap the bottle tightly and place it back in your automotive tool kit.

POWER LOSS

If your steering wheel suddenly becomes difficult to turn, don't panic. You may have run out of power steering fluid or the belt that drives the power steering fluid pump may have snapped. In either case, your mechanic should examine the car.

Though you've lost "power," you can still drive your car. It will just take some arm power to negotiate the corners between you and your mechanic's garage.

Engine Electronics

Most automobile engines built after 1986 are equipped with a computer. In automotive technology terms, it's referred to as the electronic control module (ECM) or electronic control unit (ECU). This unit usually sits behind the engine.

Sensors located throughout the engine record and feed information to the computer. Most cars have at least six sensors. One sensor monitors the temperature of the coolant; a second sensor measures the amount of oxygen in the exhaust system; a third watches braking and traction; a fourth oversees throttle position on the gas pedal; a fifth observes the transmission; and a sixth feeds back to the computer the amount and quality of air and fuel entering the fuel injectors.

Your mechanic is the most qualified person to evaluate and service the computer system in your car. She'll have the diagnostic equipment needed to to evaluate the computer and sensors and identify any problems.

High-tech doesn't mean infallible. As with other under-the-hood components, the sensors and ECU or ECM wear down over time. The vibration of your car as it traverses highways and byways, dirt and other particle buildup, and the tremendous amount of heat generated by the engine can all contribute to electronic malfunction. The telltale signs may be obvious to the driver, such as an engine that idles roughly, or so subtle that only special diagnostic equipment, such as an exhaust analyzer, can pick it up.

Emission Control Devices

With public concern growing about pollution, greenhouse gases, and global warming, automobile manufacturers have taken initiatives to make vehicles more environmentally friendly. Emission control devices are one such measure. They're designed to reduce the amount of pollution emitted from the engine and exhaust system. They're also meant to help the vehicle run more smoothly.

There are three types of emission control devices in use today: the evaporative emission control (EEC) system, the exhaust gas recirculation (EGR) system, and the positive crankcase ventilation (PVC) system.

The evaporative emission control (EEC) system traps gas vapors in a canister. These vapors are burned in the engine instead of being released into the atmosphere. The EEC is located at the front of the engine; you may see a couple of small hoses extending from it.

The exhaust gas recirculation (EGR) system sits in a round metal housing unit on the intake or exhaust manifold. This system redirects exhaust gases back to the engine for reburning. The EGR unit has a hose attached to it; if it becomes clogged with carbon deposits, the result may be poor engine idling or stalling.

The PCV system is mounted near the engine block, and it has two functions: fuel economy and pollution reduction. The PCV valve is a small component with a big job. It routes fuel fumes that escape from the engine block back into the intake manifold, where they are reburned, giving your car a little extra oomph and destroying the noxious gases before they reach the outside atmosphere.

Aside from replacing the PCV valve at the periodic intervals recommended by your car's manufacturer (see pages 94–95 for details), you won't do much tinkering with emission control devices. In fact, you may not be able to tell whether they're functioning well or not without the assistance of your mechanic. If you're interested in knowing where they are, take a look under the hood. If you can't find any of these devices, ask your mechanic to show you where they are situated.

Checking the PCV Valve

Exhaust fumes are filled with contaminants, and over time the PCV valve can become clogged. When that happens, your car idles roughly, and sometimes it won't start at all. It's easy to check whether the PCV valve is working properly, and it's a simple job to replace it.

Not every car has a PCV valve. Check your owner's manual or consult with your mechanic to determine if your car has one.

TOOLS & SUPPLIES

- Clean rag
- New PCV hose (of the same length and width as the existing hose)
- New PCV valve (of the type recommended in your owner's manual)

1 **Park the car.** Leave the engine idling.

2 **Locate the PCV valve.** In a fuel-injected car, it sits on the intake manifold or inside the valve cover (that's the top of the engine block). If you have trouble finding the valve, look for the PCV hose, which extends from the valve to another spot on the engine block. If you still

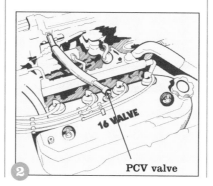

PCV valve

can't find it, consult your owner's manual.

3 **Detach the PCV hose.** The hose connects at one end to the PCV valve and at the other end to the engine block. Take care to note where it came from, because you'll have to put it back in the same place later.

4 **Clean the hose.** Use a clean rag to wipe down the outside of the hose.

5 **Test the hose.** Place your hand over one end of the hose. Take a deep breath and blow hard into the other end of the hose. Can you feel your breath coming through the hose? Does any gunk come spattering out on your hand?

➡ **If the hose seems clogged,** feels brittle, or is cracked, discard it and use the new hose.

➡ **If the hose seems fine,** put the new hose back in your tool kit; you won't need it this time.

6 **Attach the hose to the engine block.** Reattach one end of the hose (new or old) to the PCV connection on the engine block (not the valve).

7 **Remove the PCV valve.** Remove the PCV valve from its position on the valve cover or the intake manifold.

8 **Test the PCV valve.** Attach the loose end of the hose to the appropriate end of the PCV valve. Place a finger over the open end of the PCV valve.

➡ **If you feel suction,** the valve is fine — just replace it in the valve cover or the intake manifold and you're done.

➡ **If you don't feel suction,** you'll have to replace the valve. Move on to step 9.

9 **Install a new valve.** Remove the PCV valve from the hose. Pop on the new PCV valve. Then carefully push the other end of the new valve into the valve cover.

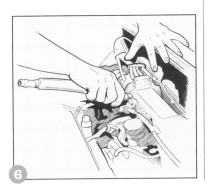

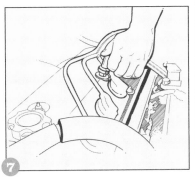

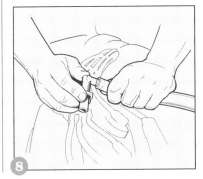

Windshield Wipers

Windshield wiper blades don't fall in the "under-the-hood" category, but windshield washer fluid does. As wiper blades deserve the same kind of maintenance attention that under-the-hood components receive, let's talk about them here.

Unfortunately, wiper blades are among those things we tend to ignore. Think of how annoying it is to be driving through a pelting rainstorm or an icy blizzard with only a small window of clear vision through your windshield. The wipers swipe noisily back and forth but seem to just float right over the streams of water or patches of ice that obscure your vision. You crane your neck up high or crouch down low in your seat so that you can see through that one small clear area. You know it's silly to be driving around like this, but you're in a hurry, there's no place to stop, or you just can't be bothered.

Silly is the right word for this. New windshield wipers are inexpensive and easy to install, and they can make a world of difference during inclement weather. If the windshield wipers currently on your car are not getting the job done, replace them! And as a precautionary measure, from now on replace the wiper blades every spring and fall.

It's easy enough to ask your mechanic to replace the wiper blades when your car is already at the garage. But it's also a simple task to perform at home. You can buy new wiper blades at any auto parts store. Wiper blades come in different lengths, so before shopping, measure the length of each front wiper blade — sometimes they're different lengths. If you have a rear wiper blade, measure it, too.

Windshield Washer Fluid

The windshield washer fluid reservoir should always be full, whether it's sun-filled summer or ice- and slush-filled winter. When you find yourself in a situation where you need washer fluid and you don't have it, you certainly regret it. Ever tried driving with your head hanging out the window?

There are two types of windshield washer fluid. Winter washer fluid is usually blue and is formulated so that it won't freeze. Summer washer

To avoid splashing washer fluid on nearby engine components, use a funnel to pour washer fluid into the washer fluid reservoir.

partment. Its cap is often white or blue, and the reservoir itself is clear. The only other clear container under the hood is the antifreeze recovery tank, which holds coolant. Coolant is green or pink. Washer fluid is blue or pink. Be sure to distinguish between the two reservoirs!

It's a good idea to keep a jug of windshield washer fluid in your trunk. When you need to top off, just flip open the cap on the reservoir and fill 'er up.

Washer Fluid Nozzles

Sometimes, even when the reservoir is full, you might not be getting enough washer fluid on the windshield. What's wrong? The nozzles that spray washer fluid onto your windshield, which are mounted on the hood of your car, may be clogged or not properly positioned. Clean the nozzles using a needle or straight pin or by blowing into the nozzle itself. If a nozzle is too clogged, you may need to ask your mechanic to replace it. To properly position the nozzles, use your fingers or a pair of pliers and cautiously twist them.

fluid is pink and is formulated to help remove dead bugs and other grimy stuff from your windshield. If you use summer washer fluid, be sure to change over to winter washer fluid before cold weather hits — if summer fluid freezes in the washer fluid reservoir, it could cause the reservoir to crack.

The windshield washer fluid reservoir is usually in one of the front corners of the engine com-

A PEEK UNDERNEATH

Some of your car's most vital innards are found not under the hood but under the car itself. To get an overview of these components, including the tires, brakes, suspension, and exhaust, one might suggest that you put on an old pair of overalls and crawl underneath. A more practical — and cleaner — solution is for you to ask your mechanic if you can take a look the next time your car is up on the garage's hydraulic hoist. From this vantage point, you'll be able to see more clearly the front, back, and all that's in between. Ask your mechanic to remove a tire, which will give you a good look at the suspension and braking systems. And while you're there, have your mechanic walk you through a quick examination of the wear and tear on all the components underneath your car. If you've read this chapter beforehand, you can follow along, nodding in affirmation.

Tires

Tires hold you and your car to the pavement through wind, rain, and snow, while cruising down the highway and when screeching to a halt, over gravelly roads and across spine-jarring potholes. How a tire handles these pressures has a lot to do with how well it was constructed.

Over the years, tire manufacturers have made extensive use of technologically advanced computer systems to analyze the forces that tires must withstand. Each different type of tire is tested at varying speeds with different weight loads and under numerous road conditions. The result is a dynamic display of new tires equipped to fit any make and model of vehicle and able to grip all types of road surfaces in all kinds of weather. The trick is choosing the tire that best suits *your* car and *your* needs.

Resisting the Advertising Onslaught

The next time you're out and about, grab a few brochures from some local tire retail outlets. They'll give you a good sense of not only how much technology influences tire manufacturing, but also the extent of marketing money that goes into promoting tires. The brochures offer a barrage of information:

DIRECTIONAL TREAD DESIGN!

BITING EDGES!

AGGRESSIVE SHOULDER TREAD BLOCKS!

PREMIUM SIDEWALL STYLING!

TREMENDOUS CORNERING FORCE!

OUTSTANDING WET TRACTION AND DRY GRIP!

SUPERB ON-CENTER FEEL!

CRISP HANDLING!

QUICK STEERING RESPONSE!

ASTOUNDING ADHERENCE AND CONTROL!

Can it all be true? Certainly. There are a lot of good-quality tires in the marketplace today. Don't forget, though, that there is also intense competition among tire manufacturers. As a smart consumer, you must become immune to the seduction of advertising. Your job is to walk into the tire retail center with the information about the type of tire that is right for your car and your driving habits already in hand. The emphasis should be on "right for your car and your driving habits." It makes no sense, for example, getting hyped up about premium all-season, high-performance radial tires when you do all your driving in warm-climate suburbia.

In making the decision to buy new tires, your financial situation is always a factor. However, don't let special promotions sway you from your research. Be on the lookout for a good deal, but buy the best tires that you can afford. Your money will be well spent.

Dissecting a Tire

A tire is simple in function yet complex in design. As a tire rolls around and around, carrying the tremendous weight of your car, incredible forces push and pull at it. To withstand these forces, the tire must be sturdy yet flexible. Rubber allows it to be both.

A flat surface tends to skid; a rough surface tends to cling. That's why a tire has treads on its surface. Treads give it some grip on the road. The number of treads and their depth, width, spacing, and shape all affect how well the tire grips the road.

Directly beneath the treads are rubber-coated cords called belts. The material that makes up the belt cords plays a large part in a tire's performance — and how much it will cost you. Finely woven thick cotton was originally used in cord construction, but steel, fiberglass, rayon, and nylon are now common.

The body of the tire is referred to as the casing. Like the belts, the casing is constructed of steel, fiberglass, rayon, or nylon cords. The casing gives the tire a rigid shape so that it continues to look like a tire — doughnut-shaped, with a flat edge around the circumference — when it's inflated.

A steel wire, called the bead, runs along the inside ring of the tire and secures it to the wheel rim. The wheel rim is a part of your car; it's the metal cylinder that sits in the center of a tire when it's mounted on your car.

Like bicycle tires, automobile tires have a valve system that allows you to add or release air from the tire. The valve extends from the tire's outside ring.

A tire's specifications — how big it is, the maximum weight it can support, its recommended air pressure, and so on — are printed on the side of the tire, known as the sidewall. For a lesson in interpreting a tire's sidewall, read on!

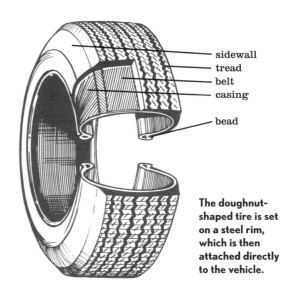

sidewall
tread
belt
casing

bead

The doughnut-shaped tire is set on a steel rim, which is then attached directly to the vehicle.

A Sidewall Translation

The jumble of letters and numbers on a sidewall can be indecipherable to the untrained eye. It is a simple matter, however, to educate yourself. Use the tire below and the following descriptions as a guide to interpreting the sidewalls on your tires.

P205/70R14 92S

P = Passenger vehicle. (*LT* would mean "light truck.")

205 = The width from sidewall to sidewall, in millimeters.

70 = Ratio of tire height to tire width.

The codes printed on a tire's sidewall give you all the information you need about that particular tire. If you can't make sense of the codes, staff at the tire center should be able to help you.

R = Radial. (*B* would mean it was bias-belted; *D* would mean it was diagonal or bias-ply; *E* would mean it was elliptic.)

14 = Diameter of the wheel rim in inches.

92 = Load index. This correlates to an industry-wide scale used to denote the weight a tire can bear.

S = Speed rating. "S," for example, indicates that the tire can support a maximum speed of 112 mph (180 kph). See the chart below for details.

SPEED RATING

Rating	Maximum Speed
Q	100 mph (160 kph)
S	112 mph (180 kph)
T	118 mph (200 kph)
U	124 mph (207 kph)
H	130 mph (217 kph)
V	149 mph (248 kph)
Z	Above 149 mph (+248 kph)

TREAD WEAR, TRACTION, AND TEMPERATURE

The letters and numbers that accompany these terms on the sidewall are codes for the Uniform Tire Quality Grading (UTQG) system. Comparing UTQG among tire brands is not useful, unfortunately, because tire manufacturers assign ratings to their tires only; there is no industry-wide scale. If you want to compare tread wear, traction, and temperature, do it within a tire manufacturer's product line.

Tread Wear 200 = The tread wear index baseline is 100. A tire with a tread wear index of 200 will last twice as long as a tire graded 100.

Traction A = The traction index rates the ability of the tire to stop on wet pavement. *A* is the highest rating and *C* the lowest.

Temperature A = The temperature index rates the tire's ability to handle heat. *A* is the highest rating and *C* the lowest.

MAX. PRESS. 32 PSI

The PSI (pounds per square inch) indicates the maximum air pressure that should be allowed in a cold tire. (It's sometimes expressed as kilopascals, or kPa.) The maximum air pressure for a tire is not the same as the *recommended* air pressure; it merely tells you what sort of air pressure the tire can withstand. For full riding comfort, maximum tire performance, and fuel efficiency, fill your tires to the air pressure recommended by your car's manufacturer. (See page 109 for more information.)

MAX. LOAD 1400 LBS

This measurement indicates the total weight, in pounds or kilograms, the tire can support when cold. This weight is especially important to note when you're taking a road trip; be sure that the weight of the passengers and luggage added to the weight of your car doesn't exceed the weight the tires can safely support.

To find out how much your car weighs, look in your car owner's manual. Use a bathroom scale to get an accurate weight on luggage and other cargo. As for determining the weight of each of your passengers — good luck!

ALL-SEASON

This particular tire is built to handle most road surfaces and weather conditions. Sometimes the "all-season" status is indicated by symbols of the four seasons molded onto the tire sidewall.

AUTOTALK

A tire should be cold when you check its air pressure, but that doesn't mean you have to wait for plummeting temperatures. While you're driving, the friction between tire and road creates heat, which warms up the tire. A cold tire is simply one that hasn't been exposed to that friction. What does this mean for you? Just that you shouldn't check tire pressure after you've been driving around, because a warm tire will give an inflated reading. (No pun intended.)

Most vehicles built today are equipped with all-season radial tires; less common are "winter" or "all-terrain" tires.

DOT

The letters *DOT* indicate that the tire has complied with the safety standards mandated by the United States **D**epartment **o**f **T**ransportation.

Following *DOT* are numbers that identify the tire; it's a serial number of sorts. If the manufacturer of your tire is recalling certain types of tires, you'll know whether your tire is in the recall category by examining this "serial number."

Tires for Winter Weather

There's a bit of controversy surrounding the use of winter radial tires. After all, if you can buy tires that work in all seasons, why would you want to use winter-only tires, which must be exchanged in warmer months for "summer" tires? The truth is, most people can get along just fine with all-season tires. Even those who live in snowy northern climates don't always need winter tires, especially if they drive mostly on major highways and city byways that are plowed quickly and regularly during snowstorms.

If you think that your driving habits and climate don't necessitate the added expense of winter tires, a more practical suggestion is to put top-quality all-season radial tires on all four wheels of your car.

Some all-season radials have silica sand mixed in with their rubber base, which gives them added traction. They're designed to handle any type of road surface, including ice- and snow-covered roads. Other all-season radials are made with, of all things, walnut shells. The theory is that walnut shells, when crushed, are harder than ice.

Whatever they're amended with, all-season radials will give you great handling all year round. As a side benefit, you won't have to go through the hassle of having your tires changed every spring and winter.

For those who live in areas that receive regular heavy snowfall and where the roads are plowed infrequently, snow tires can make a difference. How many snow tires do you need to put on your vehicle? Follow the guidelines on the next page.

- **If you have front-wheel drive,** install snow tires on the front wheels. (The weight of the engine sits at the front of a front-wheel-drive vehicle, and braking happens at the front wheels.)
- **If you have rear-wheel drive,** install snow tires on the rear wheels. (Braking occurs at the rear tires.)
- **If you have four-wheel or all-wheel drive,** install snow tires on all four wheels. (Braking takes place on all four tires.)

Wheel Balancing

Most tires, even those that come straight from the factory, have irregularities, or they develop them after being on your car for a while. To compensate for these irregularities, a tire must be *balanced*. Your mechanic will test the tire and rim, on or off your car, to see which way it wobbles. She'll then affix a small lead weight to the rim (where it touches the bead of the tire) to counterbalance any wobbling.

Balancing a tire on the car (dynamic balancing) is preferable to balancing a tire off the car (static balancing), because it takes into account the braking and suspension components that are attached to the wheel.

Wheel Alignment

On most cars, tires are set parallel to the body of the car. Jerky stop-and-start driving, driving over potholes, hitting curbs when turning and parking, and even normal wear and tear can, over time, cause your tires to tilt in or tilt out. In the world of auto mechanics, this is known as toe-in and toe-out. In laywomen's terms: Toe-in is

AUTOTALK

A wheel alignment is often called a front-end alignment, because it's the front wheels that usually need to be aligned. Some vehicles, such as those with independent rear suspension, require that the rear wheels also be aligned.

pigeon-toed, while toe-out could be likened to a Charlie Chaplan pose.

Some car owners prefer to set their front wheels with a little toe-out. Someone must have told these drivers that setting the wheels like this improves speed. It's true that race-car drivers may give their front wheels a little toe-out. However, for those of us who do not participate in the Indy 500, toe-out is simply a waste of good tire rubber. A little toe-out or toe-in isn't going to cause any harm, but if it exceeds 0.1 inch (2.5 mm), a wheel alignment should be performed.

How can you tell if your tires need to be aligned? Check the tire for unusual tread wear patterns, as described on pages 110–111. Be alert for steering difficulties, such as your car pulling to one side and taking turns sloppily. Another easy way to tell if your wheels need alignment is to drive at highway speed on a paved road in a straight line, then take your hands off the steering wheel, just for a few seconds. Your car should continue moving in a straight line. If it veers right or left, then bringing your car to the garage for a wheel alignment is probably a good idea.

Wheel alignment

Toe-out:
The wheels splay out.

Toe-in:
The wheels turn in.

Reading Tire Tread

A tire with worn or defective tread will not be able to slow or stop your car as well as it should. A car with very worn tread tire will tend to skid, regardless of weather conditions and road surfaces. There are three simple ways to check a tire's tread.

1 **The penny test.** Insert a penny head-down into the tread groove. If the top of Lincoln's head (or the Queen's head, in Canada) is visible, it's time to replace the tire.

2 **Depth gauge.** Use a tread depth gauge (available at auto parts stores) to check the depth of the tread at two different points on the tire. When the gauge reads ²⁄₃₂ inch (1.6 mm), the tire is too worn to be effective. It should be replaced and the old tire sent to the recycling center.

3 **Tread wear indicators.** Many new tires have tread wear indicators, or "wear bars," molded across two or more tread grooves. When the tire tread wears down, the tread wear indicators appear as thin flat bands running horizontally across the tire.

Tread depth gauge

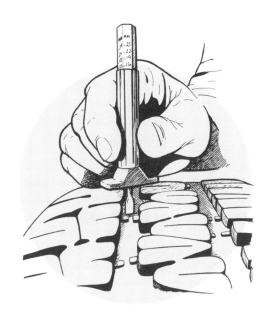

The tread depth gauge consists of a ruler inside a plastic or metal sleeve. Press the tip of the ruler into the groove between two treads and slide the sleeve down until it meets the edge of the tread. The top of the sleeve marks the measurement on the ruler that equates to the depth of the tread.

Tire Pressure

For cruising comfort, for safety, and to minimize tire repair bills, keep all your tires inflated to the pressure recommended by your vehicle's manufacturer. You can find this information in your owner's manual, on a sticker affixed to the inside of the driver's door, or on a sticker in the glove compartment. You'll want to note whether your car has different air pressure specifications for front and rear tires (some cars do, especially in rear-wheel-drive and four-wheel-drive vehicles). The recommended tire pressure will most likely fall between 28 and 32 pounds per square inch (PSI) or 192 and 220 kilopascals (kPa).

While most service-station air-pumping machines offer an air-pressure gauge, these gauges tend to be inaccurate. It's makes good sense, then, to invest in a good-quality tire pressure gauge to keep in your glove compartment. Make sure the gauge reads pounds as well as kilopascals. It should read up to 60 PSI (410 kPa) so that you can read the air pressure in your compact spare tire. (Spare tires generally have a much higher air pressure rating than do regular tires.)

AUTOTALK

A relatively recent innovation in tire technology is the smart tire. This tire contains microscopic temperature and pressure sensors that indicate when the tire is going flat or when it should be replaced. One of the goals of this new technology is to improve fuel efficiency; having underinflated tires increases a car's fuel consumption. The easy-to-read sensors help drivers monitor their tires' air pressure.

What do your treads look like?

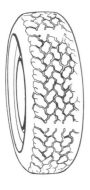

The appearance of tread wear indicators — flat bands running across the tread — indicates that the tread on a tire is worn. For safety's sake, replace any tire that shows tread wear indicators as soon as possible.

When tire treads seem cracked or worn jaggedly, the tires may need to be aligned.

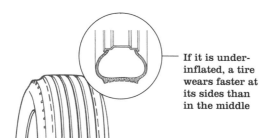

If it is under-inflated, a tire wears faster at its sides than in the middle

A tire with rapid wear at the shoulders is underinflated.

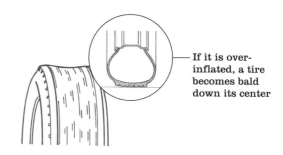

If it is over-inflated, a tire becomes bald down its center

A tire with rapid wear down its center is overinflated.

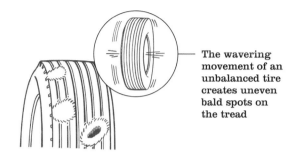

The wavering movement of an unbalanced tire creates uneven bald spots on the tread

A tire with patchy bald spots in its tread is unbalanced.

A tire with scalloped wear along one side is most likely unbalanced _and_ misaligned.

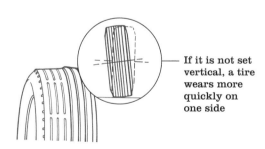

If it is not set vertical, a tire wears more quickly on one side

A tire with wear appearing on just one side has excessive _camber_ (tilt).

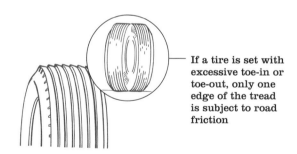

If a tire is set with excessive toe-in or toe-out, only one edge of the tread is subject to road friction

A tire whose treads are worn down to a feathered edge has excessive toe-in or toe-out.

Checking Tire Pressure

Take your car to a gas station with an air-pumping machine to check tire pressure. That way, if you find that you have to add air to a tire, you can do it right away. Tires should be cold when you check their air pressure. Tire pressure can decrease as much as 1 pound (0.5 kg) for every 10 degrees Fahrenheit (5 degrees Celcius) the temperature drops, so check the air pressure in all the tires, including the spare, every 2 weeks in autumn and winter and once a month during the warmer months.

TOOLS & SUPPLIES

- Tire pressure gauge

1 Take a look at your tire pressure gauge. One end has a rounded hood containing a small point. This is the end you push into the tire valve stem to check the air pressure and to release air from the tire. The other end of the gauge has a flat or round "ruler" extending from it. The ruler is printed with numbers corresponding to air pressure in pounds per square inch (PSI) or kilopascals (kPa).

2 Remove the cap from the valve stem of the first tire. Set the cap in a safe place — it's small and easy to misplace, especially at night.

3 Reset the gauge. Push the "ruler" of the tire pressure gauge all the way into the gauge.

4 Press the gauge against the valve. Press the rounded end of the tire pressure gauge against the exposed end of the valve stem. If you don't press it on securely, you'll hear a *whoosh* sound as air escapes from the tire. (Don't worry — you can reinflate the tire later.) This won't help you read the tire pressure, however, so try again. Each time you try, be sure to push the "ruler" back into the gauge so that you'll get an accurate reading.

5 Take a reading. Once you have the tire pressure gauge properly positioned on the top of the valve stem, so that no air is escaping, the "ruler" will pop out from the gauge. When this happens, remove the gauge and look at the ruler. The place where the ruler meets the end of the gauge marks the air pressure in your tire.

➡ **If the air pressure in the tire matches what's recommended in your owner's manual,** put the valve cap back on.

➡ **If the air pressure in the tire exceeds what's recommended in your owner's manual,** use the rounded end of the tire pressure gauge to release air from the tire.

It doesn't take much time to lose a pound of air from a tire, so stop often to recheck the pressure.

➡ **If the air pressure in the tire is less than what's recommended in your owner's manual,** you'll have to add more air. See pages 114–115 for instructions.

6 Check the remaining tires. Following steps 1 to 5, check the air pressure in the remaining three tires.

7 Check the air pressure in the spare tire. Following steps 1 to 5, check the air pressure in the spare tire. The pressure recommended for the spare will be different from that recommended for the tires on the car; check your owner's manual for details.

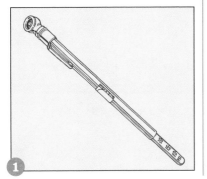

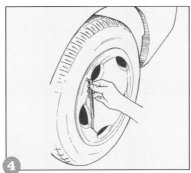

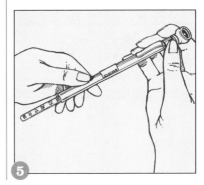

Adding Air to a Tire

To add air to a tire, you'll need an air-pumping machine. Many gas stations have one. Most air-pumping machines are coin-operated; when you feed in the proper coins, the air starts pumping, and it will keep pumping for a while — usually long enough that you can add air to at least two or three tires, if necessary.

TOOLS & SUPPLIES

- Air-pumping machine (found at many service stations)
- Tire pressure gauge

1 Examine the end of the air-pumping machine's hose. Grab the loose end of the long rubber hose that feeds from the air-pumping machine. The end of the hose has three parts: the lever, the gauge, and the feeder hose.

The lever looks like a lever-type door handle. You'll pull the lever to start the flow of air.

Just above the handle is the "ruler" of the pressure gauge. You'll be using your own gauge, so you can ignore this.

Extending from the handle just above the ruler is the short feeder hose. The end of the feeder hose looks just like the rounded end of your tire pressure gauge. This is what you'll press against the valve stem to add more air to the tire.

2 Bring the hose to the car. Untangle the hose from the air-pumping machine. Check for and straighten out any kinks. Then drop the end of the hose next to the first tire that needs to be inflated.

3 Remove valve stem caps. Remove the caps from the valve stems of all the tires that need to be inflated.

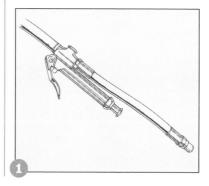

4 Start up the air-pumping machine. Go back to the air-pumping machine and feed it however many coins it requires to get the air flowing.

5 Pump air into the tire. Return to the tire. Take the end of the feeder hose and fit it directly over the tire's valve stem. As with a tire pressure

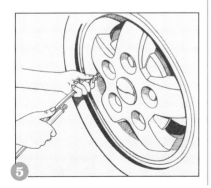

gauge, if you don't fit the end of the feeder hose securely over the valve stem, you'll hear the *whoosh* of escaping air.

6 Check the air pressure in the tire. Once you've managed to feed some air into the tire, stop to check the air pressure with your tire gauge.

7 Feed and check until the air pressure is optimal. Continue feeding air and checking the tire pressure until the tire is properly inflated according to the specifications in your owner's manual.

8 Replace the valve stem cap. Screw each cap securely on the valve stem.

9 Inflate the remaining tires. Repeat steps 3 to 8 for any other tires that need to be inflated.

10 Hang up the hose. Return the hose to the air-pumping machine, looping it neatly.

Rotating Tires

One way to ensure even tread wear — and thus a smoother ride — is to rotate your car's four tires on a regular basis. As a rule of thumb, you should ask your mechanic to rotate the tires every 5,000 to 7,000 miles (8,000–12,000 km).

The most common rotation pattern is to replace each front tire with the back tire on the same side, then put each front tire on the back wheel on the opposite side. (It's not as complicated as it sounds; see the illustration at right.) However, some front-wheel-drive cars require a different pattern of rotation. Check your owner's manual for more detailed instructions.

If your car's spare tire is a full-sized one, don't forget to include it in the rotation. You can simply swap it for one of the tires already on the car. This will ensure that all tires experience even wear. If the spare tire's tread is considerably better than the tread of the other tires when you put it on the car, your ride could become very bumpy.

If your spare tire is a compact, just have your mechanic check its tread and air pressure to make sure that it's ready for use.

Tire rotation pattern

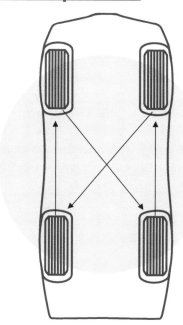

Bring your car to your mechanic to have the tires rotated. Unless you say otherwise — and you'll have to check your owner's manual to find out whether you should — your mechanic will most likely use this common pattern of rotation: The back wheels come to the front and the front wheels swap sides and move to the back.

Suspension

The suspension system gives your car some flexibility as it travels over bumps, swerves around tight corners, and stops. It also helps keep all four tires on the road and provides a smooth, safe, and stable ride for passengers and packages. Most front-wheel-drive cars built over the past few years are equipped with independent front suspension, which means that the front wheels are suspended independently of each other. Independent front suspension provides a more comfortable ride, especially over bumps and potholes, and also allows for greater ease in steering. Some newer cars have all-wheel independent suspension, which means that front and rear wheels are independently suspended.

The suspension system consists of shock absorbers or struts, springs, and a stabilizer bar. We'll take a look at them one by one.

Shocks and Struts

When you drop a rubber ball onto the floor, it doesn't bounce once and then stop, does it? No, it keeps bouncing and bouncing as it dribbles away from you. Can you imagine if tires operated the same way? They're made of rubber, after all, and they are intended to be bouncy enough that they can survive the occasional pothole and curb. But when you take on these little obstacles, your car doesn't bounce itself into infinity. Instead, it absorbs the impact and a second or two later is again on its way, returning you to a smooth, serene ride. How is your car able to do this? Through the work of its mighty shock absorbers.

Shock absorbers are a self-contained hydraulic system composed of a piston inside a fluid-filled, double-chambered cylinder. When the wheel absorbs a shock — from a bump in the road, for example — the lower chamber inside the shock is forced up inside the upper chamber, compressing the cylinder and driving the piston down. As the piston is pushed down, it displaces the fluid inside the cylinder, forcing it through a small valve. It's difficult to push a lot of liquid quickly through a small space, of course; the hydraulic fluid's resistance slows the movement of the piston, thereby dampening the shock wave and reducing the amount of bounce your car undergoes.

Shock absorber

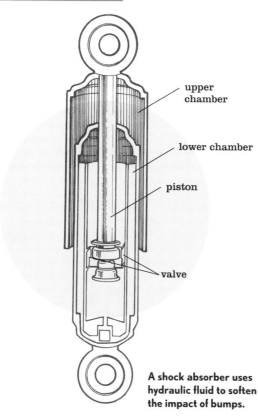

upper chamber

lower chamber

piston

valve

A shock absorber uses hydraulic fluid to soften the impact of bumps.

This whole process also works in reverse, so that your car recovers quickly and doesn't experience any "after bounces."

Most older cars employ shock absorbers, complemented by springs, between upper and lower control arms. The upper and lower control arms are horseshoe-shaped brackets called A-frames; their feet connect to the car frame, and the tip of the A contains ball joints. More formally known as ball-and-socket joints, ball joints act like rubber-encased hinges. The wheel is suspended from a spindle that connects to the ends of the upper and lower control arms; the upper ball joint and lower ball joint give the tire flexibility in up-and-down movement.

In many newer cars, however, the spring, shock absorber, spindle, and upper control arm are combined into one unit called a strut. There are two kinds of struts — rebuildable and non-rebuildable. When the shock absorber in a rebuildable strut wears down, it can be replaced. A non-rebuildable strut is sealed; when the shock absorber wears down, the entire assembly must be replaced. This, of course, makes it a more costly process.

The suspension system

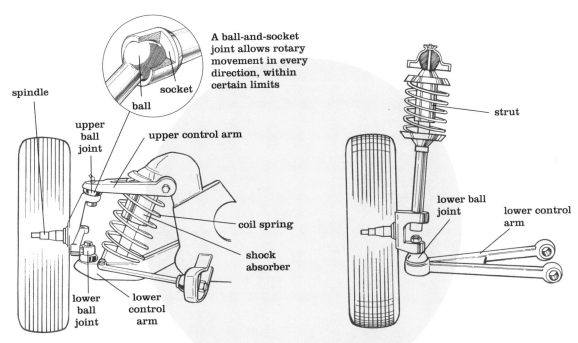

spindle

A ball-and-socket joint allows rotary movement in every direction, within certain limits

socket

ball

upper ball joint

upper control arm

coil spring

shock absorber

lower ball joint

lower control arm

strut

lower ball joint

lower control arm

In the traditional suspension system, the shock absorber is sandwiched between upper and lower control arms. Ball joints at the end of the control arms allow the tire some flexibility in up-and-down movement.

In newer cars, the suspension system combines the shock absorber, spring, spindle, and upper control arm into a single unit called the strut.

When to Replace Shocks

Unless you hit the curb at every turn or consider potholes an irresistible challenge, the shock absorbers in your car should last, on average, 100,000 miles (60,000 km). SUVs are the exception to this rule. Their extreme weight puts the suspension system under tremendous pressure, so their shocks wear down more rapidly than those in passenger cars.

There are four easy ways to determine whether the shocks (or other components of the suspension system) in your car need replacing:

1 Lean against each corner of the hood and bounce your car. If your car keeps bouncing after you have stopped, the shock absorber at that corner is probably worn out.

2 Make sure all the tires are properly inflated (see page 112), and then park your car on level ground. Have an adult sit in the driver's seat. If there is sagging at any of the car's four corners, the shock absorber at that corner may be worn out or a suspension component may be loose.

3 With your car on level ground and the engine not running, wiggle each tire back and forth using both hands. Excessive movement often indicates loose or worn-out suspension parts.

4 If your car pulls toward the last direction in which you turned (called "memory steering"), you may have a worn strut mount assembly.

If you have the front struts in your car replaced, you'll need to have your wheels realigned as well (see page 106). Always replace shock absorbers in pairs (both front shocks or both rear shocks). Why? Mismatched shock absorbers can make your car ride a little lopsided; matched shock absorbers ensure that your car is well balanced and rides smoothly.

CAUTION

Sometimes you'll see oily fluid on the shocks. While some fluid is normal, an excessive amount indicates that the hydraulic fluid is leaking from the shock absorber and the shock needs to be replaced.

Springs

Springs are a part of each wheel's suspension system. Their job is to help soften the impact of a rough road on the occupants of the car. There are four types of springs used in passenger cars: coil springs, leaf springs, torsion bars, and air springs.

Coil springs look like bedsprings and operate in much the same manner. When weight is applied to a coil spring, the spring compresses; when the weight is removed, it springs back into shape. Coil springs are often wrapped around a shock absorber, although they sometimes sit next to it.

Leaf springs are made up of a number of thin metal "leaves," or plates, laid on top of one another. When weight is applied, the leaves bend; when weight is removed, the leaves straighten. Leaf springs run parallel to the length of the vehicle's body; they are attached to the vehicle frame at either end.

Torsion bars are found mainly on SUVs. These flexible steel bars are connected to the lower control arm at the wheel. Longitudinal torsion bars run parallel to the length of the vehicle; transverse torsion bars run across the width of the vehicle,

extending from one wheel to its mate on the opposite side.

Air springs are found predominantly on luxury vehicles. They're made of rubber and filled with air. A computer sensor monitors the air pressure inside the spring, adding or releasing air to accommodate the weight being applied to the spring. Air springs provide an exceptionally smooth ride.

Types of springs

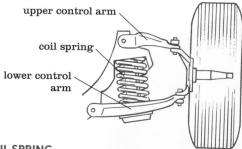

upper control arm

coil spring

lower control arm

COIL SPRING
A coil spring looks and works like bedsprings. It is usually mounted between the upper and lower control arms or is part of the strut.

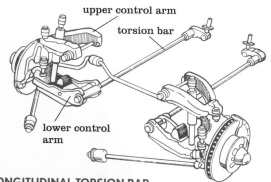

upper control arm

torsion bar

lower control arm

LONGITUDINAL TORSION BAR
A torsion bar is made of flexible steel; as it twists, it provides springlike resistance to movement.

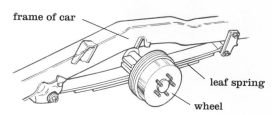

frame of car

leaf spring

wheel

LEAF SPRING
A leaf spring is a sheaf of flexible metal plates that bend and rebound to dampen bouncing. Leaf springs are most often mounted on the rear tires.

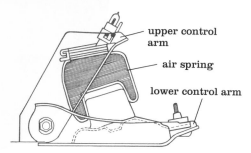

upper control arm

air spring

lower control arm

AIR SPRING
An air spring is an electronically controlled, pressurized rubber "bag" that sits between the control arms. It takes in or releases air in response to the weight applied to it.

The Stabilizer Bar

Vehicles with independent front suspension have a front stabilizer bar, which connects the suspension system at the two front wheels. Also known as the anti-sway or anti-roll bar, the stabilizer bar helps keep your car level, especially when you're making a tight turn. The bar also softens side-to-side movement.

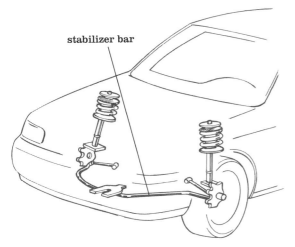

stabilizer bar

The stabilizer bar transfers force from one side of your car to the other, helping keep both front wheels on the ground when you're making a tight turn.

Some vehicles, including most SUVs, are also equipped with a rear stabilizer bar, which connects the suspension systems at the back wheels. Like the front stabilizer bar, the rear stabilizer bar helps balance your car. The extra support is often necessary for SUVs. Let's say, for example, that you happen to take a corner too tightly in your SUV, and the wheels on one side of the vehicle roll up onto the curb. In this position, your vehicle tilts to the outside. Most SUVs ride high off the ground, and they tend to be top-heavy. If the degree to which the SUV tilts is extreme, the vehicle may roll over. The rear stabilizer bar minimizes this possibility.

Notice that the operative term in our example is *minimizes*, rather than *prevents*. Drivers of SUVs and light trucks must maintain awareness of the sheer mass of their vehicles. An SUV or a light truck is not a sports car, and it shouldn't be driven like one. The tanklike enclosure of an SUV does offer increased protection to its passengers in the event of a collision, but it also can create increased dangers for those who drive recklessly.

Steering

In a nutshell, the steering system in your car transfers the motion of the steering wheel down a long shaft to a bar that connects the two front wheels. Hydraulic power makes it possible to move the wheels by a simple turn of the steering wheel.

There are two types of steering systems found in passenger vehicles: the pitman arm and the rack-and-pinion.

The Pitman Arm

The pitman arm steering system is found mostly in older cars. The steering wheel controls the steering wheel shaft, which reaches down through the engine to the pitman arm. At the connection between the steering wheel shaft and the pitman arm is a gearbox; it converts the side-to-side movement of the shaft into a pushing or pulling force on the pitman arm.

The pitman arm is attached to a long track rod, which is connected at either end to a tie rod, which is connected to a wheel. The track rod is also connected at one end to an idler arm, which is secured to the car frame. The joint between the track rod and the idler arm serves as a pivot point for the steering linkage.

Rack-and-Pinion Steering

More technologically advanced than the pitman arm system, rack-and-pinion steering makes the wheels more responsive to movements of the steering wheel. How? A long rod, called the rack, extends across the front of the car from one wheel to the other. It is scored with a series of grooves across its middle, like the ragged edge of a handsaw. The steering wheel shaft extends from the steering wheel down to the rack. The shaft ends in a pinion gear, a little cylindrical cog that is grooved like the rack. As you turn the steering wheel, the pinion gear travels across the rack, its grooves meshing with the grooves of the rack. This pulls the rack in the direction in which you turn the steering wheel.

Lubrication in a rack-and-pinion steering system is essential. The joint that connects the rack to a tie rod is packed in grease and encased in a rubber boot. Like any other rubber component, the boot can shrink, dry out, and eventually crack as your car ages. If your steering wheel becomes difficult to turn, especially when you first get on the road, it may be a sign that one of these boots is defective and the joint between the rack and the tie rod end has dried out. Your mechanic can repack the joint in grease and install a new boot to seal it.

Tie Rods

Tie rods are long metal pieces that connect the steering mechanism to the wheels. *Tie rod ends* are ball-and-socket joints that rotate as the steering unit directs the tie rods, thereby moving the wheels. Sometimes tie rod ends are encased in a grease-filled rubber boot for added flexibility.

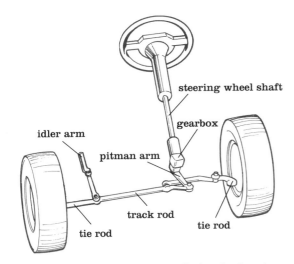

The pitman arm linkage pushes or pulls the wheels in the direction in which you turn the steering wheel.

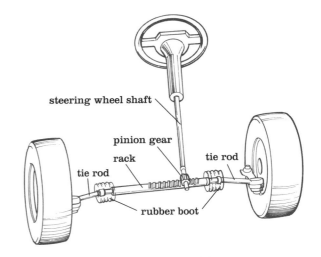

The interlocking grooves of the rack and the pinion gear pull the wheels in the direction in which you steer.

Brakes

Braking involves quite a bit more than simply applying pressure to the brake pedal. Imagine the power it takes to go from full speed to a full stop in an emergency, or even just to come to a stop at a red light. Try to stick that landing on your feet! As we've already discussed, the suspension system keeps your car's tires on the pavement. The braking system, however, does all the work of hauling back the reins on your galloping wheels.

The braking system

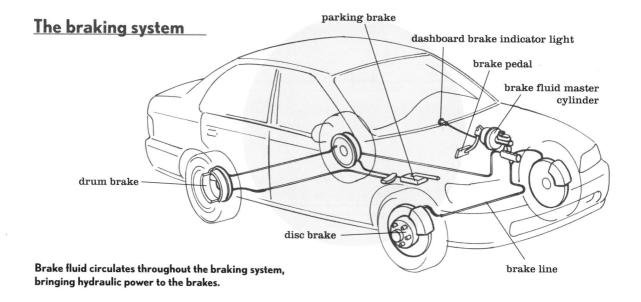

parking brake

dashboard brake indicator light

brake pedal

brake fluid master cylinder

drum brake

disc brake

brake line

Brake fluid circulates throughout the braking system, bringing hydraulic power to the brakes.

The Antilock Braking System

Many newer vehicles have what's called an antilock braking system (ABS). As a technologically advanced braking system, antilock brakes are electronically controlled and work faster than conventional brakes. The ABS engages the brakes in quick pulses, which helps keep the tires from skidding when a sudden stop is necessary.

It's important to note that the ABS is activated *not* under normal braking conditions but when there is excessive braking force — in other words, not when you just touch the brakes but when you apply steady pressure to the brake pedal. However, antilock brakes aren't a skidproof system; *nothing* can help you if you slam on the brakes while driving on a patch of ice.

Your owner's manual should indicate whether your car has antilock brakes or a conventional braking system. If your car is equipped with ABS, familiarize yourself with the antilock braking characteristics on your car, especially if you haven't driven a car with ABS before. Practice using the ABS in an empty parking lot by braking at 20 mph (30 kph). How does the brake pedal feel? What sounds do you hear coming from the brakes? How does your car move when the brakes are applied? Test your ABS under various road conditions as well, such as on ice and snow. You don't want to be caught in an unexpected driving situation and not know the braking capabilities of your car.

Turn to Stopping Suddenly (page 194) for advice on making the best use of an ABS.

AUTOTALK

Vehicles built today are equipped with a dual hydraulic braking system, which means that the front and rear wheels brake independently of each other. This way, brakes should never fully fail. You've seen that the brake fluid master cylinder has two separate compartments; one is for the front wheels and the other for the rear wheels.

Disc Brakes

Disc brakes are used on the front wheels and sometimes on all four wheels; they are never used just on the rear wheels. A disc brake is composed of two brake pads, a caliper, and a disc or rotor. The rotor connects to and spins with the hub of

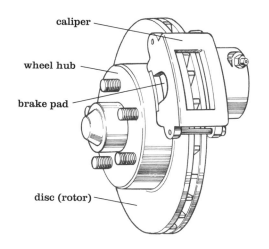

In a disc brake, the disc connects to the wheel hub. When you step on the brake pedal, the caliper squeezes brake pads against the disc.

the wheel. When the brakes are applied, the caliper squeezes the brake pads — one on either side of the rotor — against the rotor, bringing the wheel to a stop.

Disc brake pads are embedded with a *wear indicator;* it's a small piece of metal that runs partway through a brake pad and, over time and much braking, is gradually exposed. If you hear a high-pitched metallic grinding or squealing sound coming from the wheels while you drive, you're hearing the wear indicator rubbing against the rotor. This is a signal to you that the brake pads are worn down to the point where they should be replaced.

On average, disc brake pads last only about 18,000 to 28,000 miles (30,000–45,000 km), but they are not costly to replace. However, if you don't replace the pads on schedule, the calipers and rotors also begin to wear down — and they *are* expensive to replace. So stay on top of your brake maintenance schedule, and if you happen to hear the brake wear indicator sounding, replace the brake pads right away, not a few thousand miles later.

Drum Brakes

Drum brakes, unlike disc brakes, are found only on rear wheels (unless you have a pre-1970 car). The drum itself is a shallow cylinder that attaches to the wheel. Inside, two brake pads, called shoes, wrap around the inside circumference of the drum, slightly removed from the edge of the drum. When the brakes are applied, components inside the drum press outward, pushing the brake shoes against the drum and bringing the tires to a stop. Most drum brakes contain self-adjusting retractable springs that automatically move the shoes closer to the drum as the shoes wear down.

Drum brakes don't have a wear indicator that lets drivers know when a brake shoe needs to be replaced. If a drum brake shoe is worn through, you'll hear it — a grinding noise whenever you brake. If you continue driving and braking with the shoe in this condition, you'll do serious damage to the drum brake components, which will make the repair much more expensive. It would be greatly advisable, then, for you to replace those shoes *as soon as* they get to the grinding state.

On average, drum brakes last from 24,000 to 37,000 miles (40,000–60,000 km). As a precaution, have your mechanic inspect them every six months.

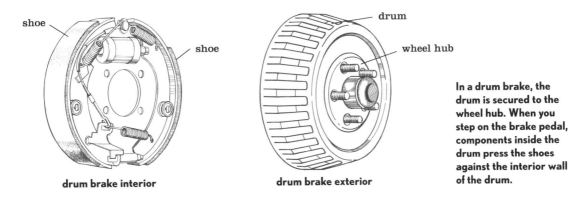

shoe

shoe

drum

wheel hub

drum brake interior

drum brake exterior

In a drum brake, the drum is secured to the wheel hub. When you step on the brake pedal, components inside the drum press the shoes against the interior wall of the drum.

How a drum brake works

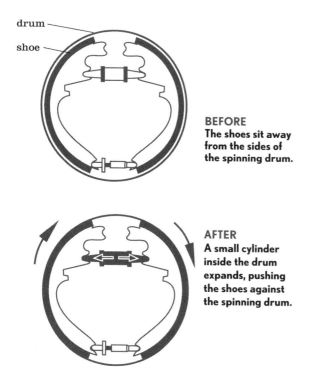

drum

shoe

BEFORE
The shoes sit away from the sides of the spinning drum.

AFTER
A small cylinder inside the drum expands, pushing the shoes against the spinning drum.

Brake Hoses and Lines

Like many automotive mechanical systems, the braking system uses hydraulics — the transmission of energy or power through the movement of a liquid. The liquid in this case is brake fluid, and it flows from the brake fluid master cylinder, which is located under the hood, through the brake lines and brake hoses to the brakes on the front and rear wheels.

Brake lines are thin steel tubes. Brake hoses are thin rubber tubes. It might seem strange that you'd need both lines and hoses to get brake fluid from one place to another. Why not just one or the other? Steel is sturdy and durable; brake lines are built to last. But rigid steel brake lines can't follow the movement of the wheels as they turn. So when the lines get 4 to 6 inches (10–15 cm) away from the brakes, they end, and the brake hoses take over, carrying brake fluid directly to the brakes. Being made of rubber, brake hoses form a flexible connection between brake lines and brakes.

Because they are exposed to the weather and attacked by salt and sand from the road, rubber brake hoses eventually crack, resulting in a fluid leak. When this happens, the braking system must be "bled," which means that your mechanic must drain all brake fluid from the system. Then she can replace the brake hoses and refill the system with new brake fluid.

The Parking Brake

The parking brake shouldn't be overlooked as part of your car's braking system. It's designed to keep your car from rolling once you've parked.

The parking brake lever is connected to the brakes on the rear wheels. When you pull up the parking brake lever, you're actually activating the rear brakes.

The parking brake cable, which runs from the lever to the rear wheels, can stretch over time. If it is not periodically tightened, the cable becomes ineffective. When is it time for the cable to be tightened? If you can drive your car with the parking brake still engaged, the parking brake cable is probably loose or broken, and you should bring your car to your mechanic for an evaluation.

AUTOTALK

Don't apply the parking brake after you've been driving in icy conditions unless it's necessary for safety. Remember, the parking brake activates the rear brakes. If ice or slush has seeped inside the rear brakes and you then activate the parking brake, the rear brakes or the parking brake cable may freeze in the "on" position. The next morning, you'll have considerable trouble moving your car; even worse, the parking brake cable may snap.

Exhaust

To understand the exhaust system, you have to get back under the hood of your car. Direct your attention to the engine block, that big massive piece of steel sitting in the center. Look closely for the exhaust manifold (see the illustration on the facing page). The exhaust manifold has long, curvy "fingers" that reach up to each cylinder's exhaust valve. The number of fingers is equal to the number of cylinders your engine has.

The exhaust manifold's "fingers" join together at the head pipe, which funnels exhaust from the engine block to the catalytic converter. The catalytic converter reburns exhaust gases to reduce pollu-tants and then sends the gases down to the muffler. The muffler "muffles" the reverberating sound of the engine that echoes down through the exhaust system and releases gases through the tailpipe. Some cars also have a resonator, which is simply a secondary muffler equipped to further reduce noise.

Exhaust components tend to rust from back to front, which is why the muffler and tailpipe are usually the first to go. How can you figure out when the muffler and tailpipe need to be replaced? You can squat down behind your car to examine the state of rust on the tailpipe; if it's excessive, bring it to the attention of your mechanic at your next tune-up. You'll recognize a rusted-out muffler when you hear it — even a small hole makes a heck of a lot of noise. If your car begins to *vroom* as loudly and deeply as a motorcycle, you probably need a new muffler.

The various exhaust pipes are attached to their respective parts by clamps and hangers. If you hear an annoying rattling sound coming from under your car, it may be that the clamps and hangers are loose. This is not yet a serious problem, but you should bring it to the attention of your mechanic.

CAUTION

A catalytic converter can get very hot in a short period of time. It's wise, then, never to park your car over dry grass, because the heat from the catalytic converter could cause a fire.

Guarding Against Carbon Monoxide

Carbon monoxide is known as a silent killer in the home, but it's a danger in automobiles as well. Loose or rusty components in the exhaust system can allow carbon monoxide fumes to seep into the interior of your car. Symptoms of carbon monoxide poisoning include drowsiness, nausea, headache, and ringing in the ears. To guard against carbon monoxide poisoning, install a small battery-operated carbon monoxide detector under one of the front seats. Check the battery every time you clean your car.

The exhaust system

The exhaust system is designed to reduce the amount of environmental pollutants — and noise — that the internal combustion engine in your car creates.

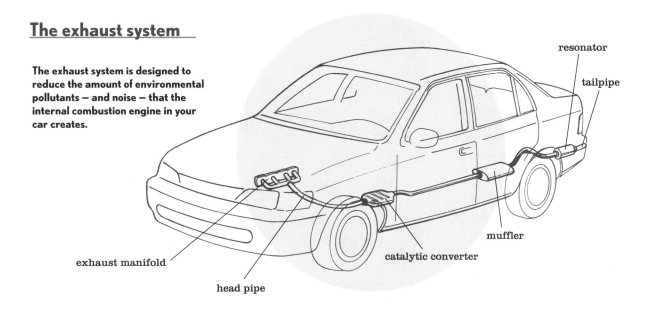

resonator

tailpipe

muffler

catalytic converter

head pipe

exhaust manifold

TROUBLESHOOTING

Without being a licensed mechanic, how can the average driver trouble-shoot unusual noises, smells, and other symptoms of an ailing car? The answer is simple: Become familiar with your own particular car. What sort of braking system does your car have? How long ago was the oil changed? What color is the coolant supposed to be?

Being able to answer these and other basic car-smarts questions will assist you in diagnosing — and often resolving — a mechanical problem. If you find that you can't figure out the problem on your own, you'll at least be confident that you can have a coherent conversation with your mechanic.

Learning to troubleshoot is like drinking a gallon of pure confidence. When your car acts up, you know what could or could not be wrong, whether the problem is minor or major, and what's the best thing to do about it so you can get your car back on the road as soon as possible.

What follows in the next few pages will help you quickly and easily identify the possible causes of automotive woes. Once you've identified a problem, you'll be able to do one of five things:

- Fix it yourself and be on your way in no time (the problem is minor and easy to remedy).
- Fix it yourself, but make an appointment with your mechanic to take your car in for further evaluation (the problem is probably minor but could signal a larger issue that your mechanic can diagnose).
- Take the car to your mechanic at your earliest convenience (the problem is not dangerous but over time can cause damage to the car).
- Immediately take the car to your mechanic (the problem is not necessarily dangerous but should be addressed right away).
- Stop driving and call a tow truck (the problem is potentially dangerous for your car and for passengers).

Responding to Indicator Lights

The indicator lights on the dashboard should light up briefly when you start your car. After a few seconds, the red lights should turn off. If one of the lights stays on or comes on while you are driving, it may mean that something is seriously wrong with your engine. Of course, it may only mean that a fuse in your car's electrical system has blown or that a wire has come loose.

When a red indicator light comes on and stays on, there are four basic steps to take:

1 Look for loose wiring.

2 Check for a burned-out fuse.

3 If it's neither a loose wire nor a burned-out fuse that's causing the indicator light to come on, check out the system that the light corresponds to.

4 If you can't find anything wrong, call your mechanic.

Look for Loose Wiring

Indicator lights are hooked up to the car's electrical system by a menagerie of wires that pass under the dashboard and connect to the fuse box. If one of these wires comes loose, it causes the indicator light it is partnered with to come on.

To take a look at the wiring, crane your neck under the steering wheel. (You may need a flashlight.) It may be difficult to establish if the wiring is malfunctioning, but you'll immediately notice if a wire is dangling or is frayed. This isn't a common problem, but it can happen. Some of the wires hang low, and your feet can pull one out without you knowing it.

If you've established that a loose or damaged wire is causing an indicator light to come on, it should be okay to drive your car. Make an appointment with your mechanic at your earliest convenience to have the wiring repaired.

Check the Fuse

No wiring problems that you can see? The next step is to check out the fuse box. If you don't know where the fuse box is, consult your owner's manual. The fuse box is usually under the dashboard near the steering wheel, although some cars have a second fuse box under the hood. It can be dark down there, so you might want to grab a flashlight.

First make sure that the ignition is turned to "off." Open the panel to the fuse box. The inside face of the panel (or your owner's manual) should have a diagram showing which fuse belongs to which electrical circuit. Find the fuse that belongs to the indicator light that is lit up.

There are two types of car fuses: thin metal prong-style fuses and European-style cylindrical glass fuses. If you have prong-style fuses, you have to pull them out of the box to look at them, using a fuse puller (see page 138). If you have glass fuses, you can examine them without removing them.

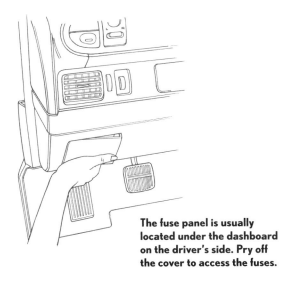

The fuse panel is usually located under the dashboard on the driver's side. Pry off the cover to access the fuses.

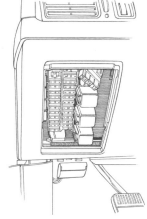

Inside the panel box is an array of fuses. Your owner's manual will tell you which of your car's electrical circuits each fuse corresponds to.

Find the fuse that corresponds to the indicator light that's staying on and examine it closely. A blown fuse is black inside or "cut" along its wiring. See the diagrams for detail.

Fuses are rated according to their capacity to carry electricity. Different electrical circuits in your car require different types of fuses. If you discover that your car has a blown fuse, you probably won't have an exact match to replace it with. Instead, put the blown fuse back into the fuse box — leaving it in place will protect the socket from dust. As soon as you possibly can, bring your car to an auto parts store. In the parking lot, remove the blown fuse. Bring the fuse into the store and have the sales staff find you a replacement.

How do you remove the blown fuse from its socket? First look for a plastic fuse puller inside the fuse box. Most cars come equipped with a fuse puller; it's usually tucked inside the fuse box. Check your owner's manual to see if you have one. You can also purchase fuse pullers at any auto parts store. In a pinch you can use tweezers with the ends covered with tissue paper. (Never allow anything metal to touch the fuse box; contact

Prong-style fuses

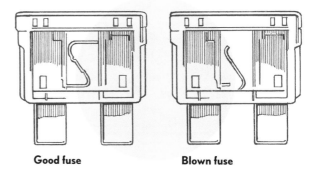

Good fuse   **Blown fuse**

Glass fuses

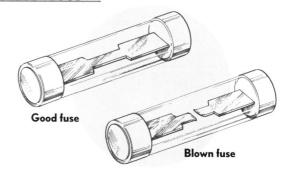

Good fuse

Blown fuse

between an electrical circuit and metal can cause an electrical short.) Simply clamp the ends of the fuse puller around the fuse and pull. Don't be afraid to put some muscle into it. The fuse box is designed to keep the fuses from coming loose, so they can be a bit sticky.

After you have replaced the fuse, be sure to replace the fuse puller and the panel that conceals the fuse box.

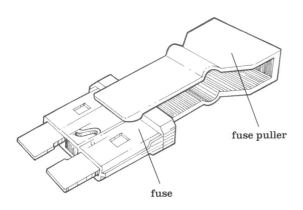

fuse puller

fuse

The fuse puller is a small plastic clip that snaps over the top of a prong-style fuse.

Evaluate the Problem

If the indicator light is *not* lit up because of loose wiring or a blown fuse, it's time to launch a full-scale investigation. In some cases you'll find the cause of the problem easily and can tackle the repair yourself. If in doubt, however, leave the work to your mechanic.

The most common problems that cause indicator lights to come on are highlighted over the following pages.

The Problem

The air bag light stays on

POSSIBLE CAUSES
- Faulty air bag
- Short circuit in the computer system

WHAT TO DO
Whether the air bag system is faulty or the computer system is out of whack, the air bag won't work — and this is dangerous. Bring your car to a local dealership at your earliest convenience. If your car is fairly new, your warranty will probably cover any repairs needed.

The Problem

The antilock brake system (ABS) light stays on

POSSIBLE CAUSES
- The ABS is activated — it's normal for the light to go on when the system is in use
- Sticking disc-brake caliper
- Low brake fluid in the brake master cylinder
- Leaking brake lines or hoses

WHAT TO DO
Open the hood and locate the brake master cylinder. If the reservoir is transparent, check to see that both compartments are filled with brake fluid; it should reach to ¼ inch (6 mm) from the top of the reservoir. If the reservoir is opaque and you need to open it to check the fluid, first wipe any dust from the top.

If the brake master cylinder is low on brake fluid, add more (see page 89 for details). If the brake master cylinder is full, there may be a slow brake fluid leak in the brake lines or hoses that won't be revealed in the master cylinder. Or, if you have disc brakes, the calipers may be malfunctioning. Immediately take the car to your mechanic to have the problem diagnosed.

The Problem

The brake indicator light stays on

BRAKE

POSSIBLE CAUSES

- Parking brake is not fully released
- Burned-out brake-light bulb
- Defective brake-failure warning switch
- Low or contaminated brake fluid
- Air locked inside brake lines
- Sticking disc-brake caliper
- Loose, frozen, or broken parking brake cable
- Leaking brake lines or hoses
- Faulty brake master cylinder
- Defective parking brake
- Deteriorated rear brake shoe

WHAT TO DO

First, make sure that the parking brake is fully released. If that doesn't help, pull over as soon as you can in a place where you can get someone to come out and look at your brake lights for you. With the engine running, step on the brake pedal and ask your helper to tell you whether both brake lights are working.

If one brake light isn't working, its bulb is probably burned out. You can replace the bulb yourself following the instructions in your owner's manual, or you can bring your car to your mechanic at your earliest convenience to have her replace it.

If none of the brake lights works, bring the car to your mechanic for an evaluation; she'll most likely need to replace the brake-failure warning switch. It's dangerous to be driving around without brake lights, so have this repair done immediately. And do *not* drive your car after dark while the brake lights are not working.

If the brake lights are working, check the amount and quality of brake fluid in the brake master cylinder. Brake fluid should rise to about ¼ inch (6 mm) from the top of the reservoir. If it doesn't, you'll need to add brake fluid (see page 89 for details).

Dip a couple of fingers in the brake fluid and rub them together. The fluid shouldn't feel gritty. If it does, bring the car to your mechanic at your earliest convenience. She'll probably "bleed" the brakes — that is, drain all the brake fluid from the car and replace it with new brake fluid.

If it's neither the brake-light bulb nor the brake fluid that's causing the brake indicator light to come on, immediately bring the car to your mechanic for a complete evaluation.

The Problem

The charge light stays on

POSSIBLE CAUSES

- Complete engine failure
- Dead or discharged battery
- Faulty alternator
- Loose wiring
- Loose or broken fan belt

WHAT TO DO

Stop the car as soon as it is safely possible. Open the hood and sniff around. Does something smell like it's burning? Don't turn the ignition back on! Call for a tow truck and get your car to your mechanic's garage right away.

If nothing smells like it's burning, inspect the battery. (Remove all jewelry from your fingers and wrists first.) Do you see white whiffs of smoke arising from the top of the battery? If so, the battery is emitting dangerous gases and you should have the car towed to your mechanic's garage.

If you don't see any signs of white smoke, open each of the vent caps and check the amount of electrolyte in the battery cells. If any of the cells are running low on electrolyte, top them off with distilled water (see page 48 for details).

Tighten the nuts that connect the battery cables to the battery. If the battery cable ends are frayed, have your mechanic replace the battery cables as soon as possible.

If the battery posts are caked with white acid buildup, they need to be cleaned. Once you've returned to the comfort of your home, prepare a solution of baking soda and water and use it to wipe down the cable ends and posts. (See page 50 for instructions).

If there's nothing wrong with the battery and you don't smell anything burning, it may be that the alternator is malfunctioning, that the fan belt is loose or has snapped, or that a loose wire under the hood is preventing electrical current from reaching or leaving the battery. The best thing to do in this case is to set up an immediate appointment to bring your car to your mechanic's garage for a complete evaluation.

The Problem

The engine light stays on

CHECK

POSSIBLE CAUSES
- Discharged battery
- Low engine oil
- Defective alternator
- Defective emissions system
- Loose or broken fan belt
- Clogged or leaking fuel line
- Incorrect grade of engine oil
- Internal oil leak in engine block
- Defective oil pump

WHAT TO DO
Check the amount of electrolyte in each of the battery cells. If any of the cells is low on electrolyte, add distilled water. If the battery posts and battery cables are caked with white acid buildup, clean them using a solution of baking soda and water when you get home. (See pages 48–51 for details on refilling and cleaning batteries.)

Check the engine oil using the oil dipstick (see page 82 for details). If necessary, top off the oil using the same weight and grade as is already in the oil pan.

If electrolyte and oil levels seem fine but the engine light stays on, it becomes potentially dangerous to the health of your car to continue driving. Although the problem could be as innocuous as a loose fan belt, it could also be as serious as a defective oil pump or a leak in the engine block. If the engine block doesn't receive adequate lubrication, it could be seriously damaged by further use. Call a tow truck and have your car brought to your mechanic's garage. The towing fees you'll be charged will be significantly less than what you might have to pay for repairs if the engine grinds itself into uselessness.

The Problem

A turn signal indicator light is malfunctioning

POSSIBLE CAUSES
- Burned-out bulb at front or rear of car
- Burned-out flasher unit

WHAT TO DO
There are two turn signal indicator lights in your car; one is for the left side of the car and one is for the right. If one signal indicator works properly but not the other, you probably have a burned-out bulb on the malfunctioning side. If both signal indicator lights come on but will not blink, you probably have a burned-out flasher unit (that's the switch that causes the signal lights at the front and rear of the car to blink).

Indicator Lights

You can replace a burned-out bulb yourself, following the instructions in your owner's manual. If you have a burned-out flasher unit, bring the car to your mechanic's garage to have it replaced.

If you are replacing a bulb yourself, keep in mind a couple of rules. First, wipe the socket with a clean rag to get rid of any dust before installing the new bulb. Second, wear gloves when touching bulbs, especially halogen bulbs, because sweat and bacteria on your hands can damage a bulb.

The Problem

**The tempera-
ture gauge
needle reaches
the red (hot)
zone**

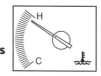

POSSIBLE CAUSES
- The engine is overheating
- The thermostat is stuck in an open or closed position

WHAT TO DO
This is a potentially dangerous situation. See When the Engine Overheats on page 210 to find out what precautions you should take to ensure that you don't end up with a car that doesn't run and needs expensive repairs.

Problems with the Brakes

Every car's brakes "feel" a little different. Over time, you grow accustomed to the way your car's brakes are supposed to feel, and you notice when they don't seem right.

There are many reasons why your car's braking system might develop problems. Some of the most common scenarios are described over the following pages. In some cases, you can correct the problem easily, but most defects in the braking system require the attention of your mechanic.

Brakes aren't a system to mess around with. They're integral to the safety of your driving experience. Although true brake failure is rare, even "loose" brakes that don't stop the car as quickly as they should can lead to a collision. They can also lead to dangerous driving habits, because when we know our brakes are starting to give out, we often try to avoid using them.

Therefore, if your brakes are acting unusually and you can't immediately identify the problem, your best course of action is to make an appointment with your mechanic to have her give the braking system a thorough evaluation.

Until then, do your best to pinpoint exactly what seems wrong. Does the brake pedal feel loose? Do the brakes grind when you apply them? Is your car skidding, even on dry surfaces? By relaying these symptoms to your mechanic, you'll give her a good head start on tracking down the problem.

Brake Problems

The brake pedal is hard to push

POSSIBLE CAUSES
- Overheated brakes
- Wet brakes
- Cracked or kinked brake hoses
- Leaking brake lines
- Faulty brake master cylinder
- Glazed (slick) disc pad or drum shoe

WHAT TO DO
Did the brake pedal become harder to push right after you rocked your car out of a snowdrift or mud pit? The repetitive pumping of the brakes may have caused them to overheat, which can make the brake pedal sticky. Try letting your car sit for 5 minutes to let the brakes cool down.

Have you recently driven through deep puddles of water? "Deep" here means 6 inches (15 cm) or more — and that isn't much water. When water gets into the brakes at the wheel, you have to apply more pressure to the brake pedal to get the brakes to work. Solve this problem by lightly applying the brakes as you drive so that the water that has accumulated inside the brakes has an opportunity to drain out.

If the brakes aren't overheated or wet but the brake pedal continues to stick, immediately bring your car to your mechanic for a diagnosis of the problem.

The brake pedal moves slowly to the floor when you stop depressing the pedal

POSSIBLE CAUSES
- Low brake fluid
- Defective brake master cylinder
- Worn-out brake disc pad or drum shoe
- Air locked inside brake system

WHAT TO DO
Pop open the hood and check the amount of brake fluid in the master cylinder. Brake fluid should rise to about ¼ inch (6 mm) from the top of the reservoir. If it doesn't, you'll need to add brake fluid (see page 89 for details).

Take a look also at the master cylinder itself. If it's cracked — you may see an actual crack or just spots of dried fluid on its outside — your mechanic will need to replace it as soon as possible.

If the brake fluid and master cylinder don't seem to be the source of the problem, immediately bring the car to your mechanic. Your front or rear brakes may be worn out, or there could be an air pocket in the brake lines somewhere. If it's the latter, your mechanic may have to bleed the brakes.

The Problem

The brake pedal feels soft or spongy

POSSIBLE CAUSES

- Faulty disc brake caliper
- Low or contaminated brake fluid
- Cracked brake hoses
- Worn-out brake lines
- Loose brake-pedal linkage
- Air locked inside brake system

WHAT TO DO

Pop open the hood and check the amount and quality of the brake fluid in the brake master cylinder. Brake fluid should rise to about ¼ inch (6 mm) from the top of the reservoir. If it doesn't, you'll need to add brake fluid (see page 89 for details).

Dip a couple of fingers in the brake fluid and rub them together. The fluid shouldn't feel gritty. If it does, bring the car to your mechanic at your earliest convenience. She'll probably have to bleed the system.

If the brake fluid seems fine, bring the car to your mechanic at your earliest convenience for a diagnosis.

The Problem

The brake pedal sticks when you brake

POSSIBLE CAUSES

- Worn-out brake hoses
- Sticky brake-pedal linkage

WHAT TO DO

When you apply the brakes and then release your foot from the pedal, the pedal should rise to its original position. If the pedal sticks — if it doesn't rise back up — you have a potentially serious problem on your hands. Immediately bring the car to your mechanic for diagnosis and repair.

Brake Problems

The Problem

The brake pedal vibrates when you brake

POSSIBLE CAUSES
- The antilock brake system (ABS) is activated — vibration in this situation is usually normal
- Warped disc brake rotor
- Defective drum brake
- Cracked brake hoses

WHAT TO DO
This situation offers a great example of how important it is to be familiar with the car you are driving. In many cars, vibration is normal when you brake hard enough to activate the ABS. However, if this vibration is not normal, you're facing a potentially dangerous situation. The braking system in your car could have defective parts. If you don't take the necessary precautions (meaning, get your car into your mechanic's garage as soon as possible), you put yourself at risk every time you get behind the wheel.

The Problem

The brakes squeak

POSSIBLE CAUSES
- The squeaking is normal — some disc brakes squeak "just because"
- Improperly installed brakes
- Clogged brake lines
- Defective brake part (such as drum shoes, plates, or springs)
- Disc-brake wear indicator is indicating disc brake pads are thin

WHAT TO DO
Here is another example of how knowing your car can help you rule out problems. Do you have disc brakes? Some disc brakes squeak as a matter of course; there's nothing wrong with them. If the squeaking is new or sounds different, it could be that the metal wear indicator in the disc brake is rubbing against the rotor; this is a signal to you that it's time to have the brake pads replaced. (See page 128 for details.)

If you've recently had new brakes installed on your car and they're squeaking, they may not have been installed properly. Bring your car back to your mechanic and have her examine them. If she tells you that they're fine, then get familiar with the squeaking — that's the new "normal" sound of your brakes.

As a general rule, if your car's brakes start to squeak, or if the squeaking sound that they normally make changes in tone, pitch, or frequency, immediately bring the car to your mechanic for an evaluation of the braking system.

The Problem

There's a thumping sound underneath your car when you brake

POSSIBLE CAUSES
- Worn-out ball joint
- Defective shock absorber
- Worn-out U-joint

WHAT TO DO

Ball joints, shock absorbers, and U-joints are parts of the suspension system. If any of them is defective (such as a ball joint drying out and cracking), your car won't be able to move. The thumping sound tells you that one of these parts is at the cusp of not working. Rather than risk expensive damage to your car, pull over to the side of the road and call a tow truck. Ask to have your car brought to your mechanic's garage.

The Problem

The interior dome light comes on when you brake

POSSIBLE CAUSE
- Blown fuse

WHAT TO DO

This is one of those strange, cross-wiring electrical phenomena. If the interior dome light comes on when you brake, it probably means that the dome light fuse is blown. At your earliest convenience, replace the fuse for the dome light. (See page 136 for advice on changing a fuse.)

The Problem

The car pulls to one side when you brake

POSSIBLE CAUSES
- Incorrect air pressure in one tire
- Wet brakes
- Improper wheel alignment
- Loose or sticky disc brake caliper
- Worn-out brake hoses or lines
- Contaminated brake fluid
- Defective shock absorber

WHAT TO DO

A car doesn't suddenly begin pulling to one side when you brake. It's a progressive problem that becomes worse and worse over time. When the car pulls to one side enough to catch your attention, the cause of the problem has existed for some time already.

Check the air pressure in all your tires; see the instructions on page 112 for details. If all the tires have an adequate amount of air, make an appointment to bring the car to your mechanic at your earliest convenience. The longer you wait to have this problem fixed, the more pronounced the pulling will be — and the more dangerous it becomes.

Scary Sounds

An unexpected noise coming from your car can often set you into panic mode. While an abrupt thumping often indicates that one of the tires is flat, other sounds are more subtle or, in many instances, simply annoying. Whether alarming or irritating, unusual automotive noises are a signal that there's something wrong with your car.

If you're on the road when a strange noise suddenly starts up, pull over. If you're in your driveway, stay put. From this safe vantage point you can begin to diagnose the problem, with the help of the tips given over the following pages.

The noises we'll discuss can be divided up into six categories:
- Strange sounds when you start up the engine
- Strange sounds from under the hood while you're driving
- Strange sounds from underneath the car (including the tires) while you're driving
- Strange sounds when you brake
- Strange sounds from the rear end of the car
- Strange sounds from accessories

Okay now. Take a deep breath. Remember, a strange automotive noise is a symptom of another problem, not a problem itself. And you *will* be able to resolve it.

Start-Up Sounds

The Sound

Clicking from the engine when the car is started up

POSSIBLE CAUSES
- Discharged battery
- Corroded or frayed battery cables
- Low engine oil
- Incorrect grade of engine oil
- Defective alternator
- Loose alternator belt
- Defective starter
- Cracked or corroded distributor cap
- Faulty spark plug wire(s)
- Loose wire between ignition switch and starter

WHAT TO DO
If the engine clicks and won't start, the battery is most likely the culprit. Is the charge indicator light on? When you turn the key in the ignition, all the indicator lights should come on briefly. If the charge light stays red after the other indicator lights have turned off, it's a sure sign that your battery isn't sufficiently juiced up.

Pop open the hood, put on a pair of gloves, and examine the battery. Are the cable ends and battery posts covered with crusty white acid buildup? If so, clean them, following the instructions on page 50. If you don't have the necessary supplies for cleaning the battery, just take a clean rag and wipe around the posts and cables.

Try to wiggle the cables. If they're loose, grab a wrench and tighten the fittings that secure the cables to the battery.

Now try to start your car. If it starts up, celebrate, but also know that you need to practice better battery maintenance. If your car won't start, try jump-starting it. If the car still won't start, no amount of cursing or cajoling will get the engine revving. Call your mechanic to set up an immediate appointment, and call a tow truck to bring your car to the garage.

If the engine clicks but will start up, you most likely have a problem developing in your car's electrical or ignition system. An immediate appointment with your mechanic makes it less likely that you'll be caught stranded with a car that just *click-click-click*s when you try to start it up.

On *rare* occasions a clicking noise from the engine could signal that there isn't enough oil in the engine to lubricate all of its parts; as dry pistons grate against the metal engine block, they click. Check the oil (see page 82 for details) and add more oil if necessary. The clicking noise could also signal that the engine oil in your car is of the incorrect grade. However, if you don't know what kind of oil was last put in the engine, it will be impossible to know if this is the cause of the clicking.

If you can't figure out what is causing the clicking noise, make an immediate appointment with your mechanic so that she can examine your car.

The Sound

No noise when you turn the key in the ignition — just dead silence

POSSIBLE CAUSES

- The transmission is not in the "park" mode (in automatics) or the "neutral" mode (in manuals)
- Driver's seat belt not engaged
- Discharged or dead battery
- Loose battery cables
- Blown fuse or fusible link
- Faulty alternator
- Defective ignition switch or wire
- Faulty starter or starter solenoid

WHAT TO DO

It happens. Usually when you're in a hurry. You hop into the driver's seat, put the key in the ignition, turn it, and — nothing. No sound of the engine turning over.

What do you do? First, don't panic! Check that the gearshift is set to the appropriate gear: "P" (for "park") in vehicles with automatic transmissions and "N" (for "neutral") in vehicles with manual transmissions. Is your seat belt on? In some cars, the engine won't start if the driver's seat belt isn't engaged.

If you've ruled out these two potential causes — and they are common — there may be a problem with the electrical or ignition system. Pop open the hood, remove all jewelry from your hands, and put on a pair of gloves. First look at the battery. Wiggle the cables, holding them close to the battery but not touching the cable ends or battery posts. Are

the cable ends loose? If so, get out a wrench and tighten the fittings that hold the cables to the battery. Are the cable ends crusted with acid buildup? If so, clean them, following the instructions on page 50. If you're far from home and don't have the time or materials to clean them, wiggling them may have loosened enough of the crusty buildup for your car to start; clean the cables when you get home.

Also check the electrolyte levels in the battery (see page 48 for details), and, if necessary, add distilled water.

If none of these efforts works, try jump-starting the battery. (To learn how, see page 208.) No luck? Perhaps the alternator is burned out or the starter has died. Maybe one of the ignition wires has come loose. Whatever the case, you'll need help. Have your car towed to your mechanic's garage.

The Sound

Whining from under the hood when you start up the car, but not when you're driving

POSSIBLE CAUSE
• Low transmission fluid

WHAT TO DO

While the noise may stop once you put the engine in gear, the problem hasn't magically resolved itself. If the transmission fluid is low, the transmission gears will be dry when you start up the car, and they'll whine as they rub against each other. As the car warms up, the fluid makes its way from the pan to the gears, and so the noise stops.

To prevent the noise from happening, and to preserve your transmission, check and top off the transmission fluid, following the instructions on page 62.

The Sound

Whirring when you try to start up the car

POSSIBLE CAUSES
• Defective driveshaft
• Defective starter

WHAT TO DO

If you hear a whirring noise while you're trying to start up your car and, in fact, your car does start up, count yourself fortunate — and make an immediate appointment with your mechanic for an evaluation of your car. The starter is a tricky mechanical part. It will tease you by giving the engine just enough juice to get going — this time. The next time you try to start up the car, it may decide not to play dead but to *be* dead.

The noise could also be coming from the driveshaft. If the driveshaft is broken and you continue to drive, it may just whir itself out of commission. It then will be an expensive affair to get your car up and running again.

So the best course of action when you hear a whirring noise coming from the engine when you're trying to start up the car is to make an immediate appointment with your mechanic.

ACT IT OUT

Whirring. Whining. Pinging. Squealing. If you can't tell one from the other, imitate it. You may feel silly clicking or hissing in your mechanic's office, and you may give her a good chuckle, but honestly, sometimes it's the only proper way to describe an automotive ailment.

Under-the-Hood Sounds

Hissing from the radiator

POSSIBLE CAUSES
- Faulty radiator cap
- Small leak in radiator core

WHAT TO DO
While this sound may not be noticeable when you're driving, once you stop, the *hiss* may attract your attention.

Pull over to the side of the road. Before opening the hood, get close to where the radiator is and listen. If the sound is loud, it signals a potentially explosive situation. Leave everything alone and call for a tow truck. If the sound isn't that loud (this is your call; if you are in any way nervous about opening the hood, don't), pop open the hood. Then find a comfortable spot on the roadside and have a sandwich or read a book. When the hissing has subsided and the radiator is cooled off, put on a pair of gloves and very carefully open the radiator cap, following the instructions on page 66.

Check for wet spots on the radiator core, which could signal a coolant leak. Look from both over and under the radiator. If you spot a major leak, you'll have to have the radiator repaired or replaced before you drive any farther, so call for a tow truck.

Examine the radiator cap for cracks and other defects. Wipe away any moisture from it. Most radiator caps have a rubber gasket that seals the joint between the cap and the radiator. If the rubber gasket is cracked, it can't provide a proper seal. Put back the faulty cap and drive to the nearest auto parts store, where you can purchase a replacement. When you go into the store, bring the faulty radiator cap with you, so that you can be sure to get the right type. You may want to consider purchasing a new radiator cap with a pressure-release device; consult with your mechanic or the staff at the auto parts store for advice.

If the radiator cap and the radiator seem to be fine, check the level of coolant, following the instructions on page 70, and top off, if necessary. Start up the engine and let it run for about 2 minutes. Then check the level of coolant again. If it has dropped, it's not safe to drive your car — call for a tow truck. If it still seems fine, it should be okay to drive your car, but make an immediate appointment with your mechanic for a thorough evaluation of the cooling system.

If the radiator starts to hiss again before you've made it to your mechanic's garage, stop and call for a tow truck.

The Sound

Pinging from under the hood

POSSIBLE CAUSES
- Broken belt
- Low engine oil
- Incorrect grade of engine oil
- Stuck emission control system(s)
- Bad gas
- Incorrect gas octane rating
- Faulty pistons
- Incorrectly gapped spark plug(s)

WHAT TO DO

Ping-ping-ping. If your car has ever made this noise, you'll know what we're talking about here. It sounds like metal clicking against metal, which could be exactly what's happening. If your car's engine has very little engine oil, the pistons inside the engine block aren't getting enough lubrication — hence the pinging. If you hear a pinging noise coming from under the hood while you're driving, immediately stop your car and check the oil (see page 82 for details).

Did you just fill up the fuel tank? Bad gas could be the cause of the pinging. Pour a bottle of fuel additive into the tank, following the instructions on the product label. If the car has bad gas, the pinging should stop shortly, as soon as the additive begins to move through the fuel system. Refuel the car, even if it's only a couple of dollars' worth, just to get good gas into the fuel system.

Did you just have the car in for a tune-up that included having the spark plugs changed? Spark plugs that were incorrectly gapped won't create enough electrical spark to keep the engine running smoothly. *Ping-ping-ping* — there's that sound again. New spark plugs come pre-gapped, and sometimes, thinking the gap is correct, a mechanic will install the new spark plugs without double-checking the gapping. If you've just had the spark plugs changed and now you hear a pinging noise from the engine, get your car back into your mechanic's shop so that she can inspect the gap on all the spark plugs.

The Sound

Rough idling

POSSIBLE CAUSES

- Bad gas
- Dirt or water in fuel tank
- Dirty air filter
- Low automatic transmission fluid
- Worn-out belt
- Damp distributor cap
- Defective emission control system
- Bent or clogged muffler or tailpipe
- Clogged fuel filter
- Dirty fuel injectors
- Leaking or kinked hose
- Improperly gapped or dirty spark plug
- Frayed or loose spark plug wire

WHAT TO DO

If your engine idles roughly, it's not operating at full efficiency, and whatever component is the culprit could be en route to a major malfunction. You can either continue to let your car idle the way it is or work at solving the problem, on your own or with the assistance of your mechanic.

Did you just fill up the fuel tank? Bad gas could be the reason that your car is idling roughly, and the car will continue to run roughly until that gas is used up. You can help ease the transition by pouring a bottle of fuel additive into the tank, following the instructions on the product label.

Do you often drive until the fuel tank is almost empty? A tank that is almost empty encourages the formation of water droplets; water and gas don't mix well, and this combi-

nation can cause your car's engine to idle roughly. From now on, fill up the tank regularly, never letting the fuel gauge needle drop below the halfway mark.

If you've ruled out bad gas and water droplets in the gas tank as causes of the rough idling, open the hood and check the following:

- **Air filter.** Is the air filter overdue for replacement? Is it so dirty that dust falls out as soon as you remove the filter from the cleaner? If so, replace it with a new filter. See page 40 for more details.
- **Fan belt.** If your car has a fan belt, take a look at it. It should be snug, meaning that it gives about ½ inch (1 cm) when you press two fingers on it. If it feels loose or tight, have your mechanic adjust it. If it is cracked or frayed, have your mechanic replace it. See page 72 for more details.

- **Distributor cap.** If your car has a distributor cap, remove it and check for cracks (even a hairline crack will cause the engine to idle roughly). See page 206 for more details.
- **Hoses.** Visually inspect hoses, such as the upper and lower radiator hoses, for cracks and frayed or leaking ends. If any of the hoses are defective, have your mechanic replace them.

TAKE NOTES

When you're waiting for a tow truck, use the time to jot down notes about your ailing car's symptoms. In addition, make note of how fast you were going when the problem started and how far you drove before pulling over.

- **Spark plug wires.** Make sure all the spark plug wires are attached to their respective spark plugs. (Wear rubber gloves so you don't get a shock.) If the wires are frayed at their ends, have your mechanic replace them.

If you can rule out these under-the-hood components, walk around to the back of the car and take a peek underneath. Does the muffler or tailpipe have holes or excessive rust? If so, you may have just diagnosed the problem. Make an appointment with your mechanic so she can further inspect these exhaust system components.

If you can't figure out why your car is idling roughly, bring it to your mechanic at your earliest convenience for a diagnosis. Once you know what the problem is, you can decide whether to have it fixed right away.

The Sound

Snapping from under the hood

POSSIBLE CAUSE
- Loose spark plug wire

WHAT TO DO
When you hear what sounds like rubber slapping against something, the rubber boot (that's what the end of the spark plug is called) may be disconnected from its respective spark plug. Pop open the hood and put on a pair of rubber gloves. Inspect all the spark plug wires, making sure that they fit snugly onto the spark plugs and that they aren't frayed anywhere along their length. If there is any exposed wiring, do not touch it, and make an immediate appointment with your mechanic to have the wire replaced.

Squealing from under the hood

POSSIBLE CAUSES

- Bent air cleaner cover
- Low fluid in power steering reservoir
- Faulty radiator cap
- Loose or worn-out belt
- Faulty alternator
- Faulty water pump

WHAT TO DO

To replace an air filter, you must open the air cleaner, pull out the old filter, install a new filter, and then cinch down tight the cover of the air cleaner. Over time, this periodic loosening and tightening of the air cleaner cover can cause it to warp out of shape. If the cover warps badly enough that it doesn't create a tight seal with the bottom of the air cleaner, air escaping through the resulting crack makes a squealing or whistling sound. If you can determine that the squealing is coming from your air cleaner, you may be able to reshape the cover so that it provides a tighter fit, but you'll mostly likely have to decide whether to continue listening to the squealing or make the investment and purchase another air cleaner cover for your particular make and model of car.

Another source to check is the power steering fluid reservoir. Low levels of power steering fluid could cause steering components to dry out, so that they "squeal" to be lubricated. Check the level of fluid in the reservoir, following the instructions on page 90, and top off if necessary.

The squealing noise could also be coming from the radiator cap. When your car is warmed up, the cooling system becomes pressurized. If the radiator cap is not providing a tight seal on top of the radiator, you may hear a squealing or hissing noise. Radiator caps are inexpensive, so it's a good idea to purchase a new one and install it in your car to see if the noise stops before you go ahead and make an appointment with your mechanic for a checkup.

If the noise persists despite the new radiator cap, bring the car to your mechanic at your earliest convenience.

The Sound

Ticking from under the hood when the car is idling

POSSIBLE CAUSES
- Low engine oil
- Faulty valve in engine block

WHAT TO DO

Call it a *ping,* call it a *tick* — when metal rubs against metal, you'll hear it. Like pinging, described on page 155, ticking usually is a symptom of insufficient lubrication. Pull over to the side of the road and let the engine cool. Then check the oil (see page 82), topping off if necessary.

If the level of oil seems fine, there may be a faulty valve in the engine block that's obstructing the flow of oil. Make an immediate appointment with your mechanic to have the problem diagnosed; lack of oil can cause the engine to overheat, which can be a serious problem.

The Sound

Whistling when the engine is running

POSSIBLE CAUSES
- Clogged air filter
- Loose fan belt
- Broken or disconnected hose
- Vacuum hose leak
- Malfunctioning positive crankcase ventilation (PCV) valve
- Leak in engine vacuum seal

WHAT TO DO

You should be able to determine the cause of this noise on your own. Open the air cleaner and visually examine the air filter, following the instructions on page 40.

Check your owner's manual to find out how often the air filter needs to be changed, and if you're overdue, replace it.

If your car has a fan belt, take a look at it. It should be snug, meaning that it gives only about ½ inch (1 cm) when you press on it with two fingers. If it feels loose, have your mechanic tighten it. If it's cracked or frayed, have your mechanic replace it.

Examine each of the hoses in turn. Look for cracks in the hose lining, and trace each hose to its end to make sure it is securely connected. If a hose has become disconnected, clamp it back in place. If it's cracked, have your mechanic replace it.

If none of the above steps solves the problem, take a look at the PCV valve. If necessary, replace it. (See page 94 for details.)

If you can't identify the problem, you may have an air leak in the engine block. The pistons dropping through the cylinders create a sucking vacuum seal; if there's a leak, the pull of air into the cylinder will make a whistling noise. Ask your mechanic to evaluate the problem.

Sounds from Below

The Sound

Clunking sound (and feeling) underneath the car when you are shifting gears

POSSIBLE CAUSES
- Slipping transmission gears
- Loose CV-joint
- Low or dirty transmission fluid
- Defective U-joint

WHAT TO DO
Clunking noises when you shift gears are a potential signal of transmission problems. Unfortunately, transmission repairs are often complex and expensive. However, the longer you wait, the bigger the problem becomes. Check the transmission fluid, following the instructions on page 62, and top off with more fluid if necessary, but also make an appointment with your mechanic for a complete evaluation.

The Sound

Grinding from the wheels

POSSIBLE CAUSES
- The disc-brake wear indicator is letting you know brake pads are worn thin
- Worn-out or dry wheel bearing

WHAT TO DO
As is most often the case, the longer you wait, the more expensive this repair is going to be. Whether it's the disc brakes that need replacement or the wheel bearings that need to be greased, the problem needs a mechanic's attention. Make an appointment to take the car to your mechanic's garage as soon as possible.

The Sound

Knocking or clicking from a front wheel when the car is turning a corner

POSSIBLE CAUSES
- Cracked boot covering on CV-joint
- Worn-out strut mount assembly

WHAT TO DO
When you hear a clicking or knocking from a front wheel as you turn a corner, there's probably a problem with your front-end suspension. Repairing or replacing suspension parts is expensive, and the longer you drive your car with malfunctioning suspension, the more expensive the repair is likely to be. Bring the car to your mechanic at your earliest convenience for a complete diagnosis.

Rattling from around a tire

POSSIBLE CAUSES
- Stone, pebble, or other object lodged between hubcap and tire
- Incorrectly installed disc brake pads
- Worn-out or missing brake parts

WHAT TO DO
Because the cause of this noise could be linked to defective brakes, it's important to evaluate the problem immediately. First eliminate the possibility that a small rock is lodged between the hubcaps and the tire. Remove the hubcap from all four wheels (the instructions for changing a tire on page 200 will show you how to remove a hubcap). Feel all around the inner wall of each tire, making sure that a tiny pebble doesn't go undiscovered. If you find a pebble, discard it and put the hubcap back on. When you're done, get back on the road. If you don't hear a rattling, you've solved the problem. If the rattling continues, you may have a problem with the brakes. Immediately take your car to your mechanic's shop.

The Sound

Rattling from underneath the car

POSSIBLE CAUSES
- Deteriorating exhaust part (such as the muffler or tailpipe)
- Loose or broken hangers and clamps along the exhaust system

WHAT TO DO
A deteriorating exhaust system is potentially dangerous; rusted-out parts can leak carbon monoxide fumes into the interior of your car. Broken hangers and clamps, on the other hand, are relatively innocu-ous, and they're inexpensive to repair. Whatever the cause of the noise, you'll need your mechanic's help to fix it. Make an appointment to bring your car into her shop as soon as possible.

The Sound

Scrunching or thunking when you drive across bumps or potholes

POSSIBLE CAUSES
- Worn-out shock absorber
- Broken spring or other suspension component

WHAT TO DO
A worn-out shock absorber won't prevent you from driving. But it can give you a headache — literally. You'll be bouncing around so much in the driver's seat that once you've stopped the car, you'll probably continue to bounce, in your

head at least. A broken spring, on the other hand, has the potential to cause serious suspension problems. Bring your car to your mechanic's garage at your earliest convenience for a diagnosis.

The Sound

Thumping from a tire

POSSIBLE CAUSES
- Flat tire
- Incorrect air pressure in one tire
- Improper wheel balance
- Improper wheel alignment

WHAT TO DO
Tires have to withstand a lot of abuse as they carry you, spinning madly, over highways and byways. One way they tell you something is wrong is by thumping.

A sudden thumping noise accompanied by difficulty in steer-ing signals a flat tire. Pull over to the side of the road as soon as it is safely possible, and turn to page 200 for advice on when and how to change a tire.

A subtle thumping noise could indicate that one or more tires is low on air. Test the air pressure in all four tires, following the instructions on page 112, and add more air if necessary. If tire pressure doesn't seem to be be the problem, improper wheel balance or wheel alignment may be the reason your tires are "talking" to you this way. Set up an appointment with your mechanic to get this problem resolved before you end up with a flat tire.

The Sound

Thumping from underneath the car when you press down on the gas pedal

POSSIBLE CAUSES
- Worn-out ball joints
- Defective shock absorber
- Worn-out U-joint

WHAT TO DO
All the possible causes of this problem are linked to the suspension system. The malfunctioning of one suspension part soon leads to undue wear and tear on other suspension parts. At your earliest convenience, ask your mechanic to evaluate all the components of your car's suspension system.

Strange Sounds When You Brake

The Sound

Squeaking brakes

POSSIBLE CAUSES
- The squeaking is normal — some disc brakes squeak "just because"
- Improperly installed brakes
- Clogged brake lines
- Defective brake parts (such as drum shoes, plates, and springs)
- Disc-brake wear indicator is indicating disc brake pads are thin

WHAT TO DO
In a case like this, knowing your car can help you rule out problems. If you have disc brakes, they may squeak a bit all the time; there's nothing wrong with them. If the squeaking is new or sounds different, it could be that the metal wear indicator in the disc brake is rubbing against the rotor. This is a signal to you that it's time to have the brake pads replaced. (See page 128 for details.)

If you've recently had new brakes installed on your car and they're squeaking, they might not have been installed properly. Bring the car back to your mechanic and have her examine them. If she tells you that they're fine, then get familiar with the squeaking — that's the new "normal" sound of your brakes.

As a general rule, if your car's brakes start to squeak, or if the squeaking sound that they normally make changes in tone, pitch, or frequency, bring the car immediately to your mechanic for an evaluation of the braking system.

The Sound

Thumping from underneath the car when you brake

POSSIBLE CAUSES
- Worn-out ball joints
- Defective shock absorber
- Worn-out U-joint

WHAT TO DO
Ball joint, shock absorbers, and U-joints are vital to the operation of your car. That thumping sound may be telling you that one of these parts is almost to the point of complete malfunction. Pull over to the side of the road and call to have your car towed to your mechanic's garage.

Strange Sounds from the Rear End

The Sound

Backfiring

POSSIBLE CAUSES
- Bad gas
- Incorrect air-fuel mixture being fed to the engine
- Low or contaminated automatic transmission fluid
- Damp or cracked distributor cap
- Clogged fuel filter
- Hole(s) in muffler or tailpipe
- Dirty or incorrectly gapped spark plug(s)

WHAT TO DO
Did the backfiring start soon after you filled up the gas tank? If so, you may have a tank full of bad gas. Purchase a bottle of fuel additive and pour it into your tank, following the instructions on the product label. If the car has bad gas, the backfiring should cease as soon as the additive begins to flow through the fuel system. To get some good gas in the system, refuel — at a different gas station! — even if it's only a couple of dollars' worth of gas.

Also check the automatic transmission fluid, following the instructions on page 62. If the reservoir seems to be running low, add more fluid. If the level of fluid in the reservoir seems adequate, use your fingers to wipe some of the fluid from the end of the dipstick. Rub your fingers together. Does the fluid feel gritty? If so, it's contaminated, and you'll have to bring the car to your mechanic at your earliest convenience for an evaluation.

If neither bad gas nor low or contaminated automatic transmission fluid is causing the backfiring, bring the problem to the attention of your mechanic at your earliest convenience.

The Sound

Howling from the rear of your car

POSSIBLE CAUSES
- Worn-out rear differential
- Low fluid level in the rear differential

WHAT TO DO
If the rear differential in your car conks out, you'll know it. Your car will come to such a dead halt you'd think you hit a brick wall. That howling sound serves as a warning that the differential is traveling the path toward deterioration. You won't be able to fix this problem yourself, so pull over to the side of the road and call for a tow truck. Have the car towed straight to your mechanic's garage.

The Sound

Rattling from the back of the car

POSSIBLE CAUSES
- Loose license plate
- Loose trunk latch

WHAT TO DO
Weird automotive noises are often frightening because they bring visions of a major repair bill. In this case, however, the racket is nothing to be afraid of. If one of the screws that secures the license plate has come loose, the plate will bang and rattle against the rear of your car. If you own a minivan or other vehicle with a rear hatch and that hatch is not secured, it will rattle as you drive. The solutions are simple: Tighten all the screws holding the license plate and open and close, once again, the back hatch on your vehicle.

The Sound

Rumbling or spitting from the rear of the car

POSSIBLE CAUSE
- Exhaust leak

WHAT TO DO
If your car starts to sound like a motorcycle, you have an exhaust leak. Bring the car to your mechanic at your earliest convenience for an evaluation of the exhaust system.

The Sound

Scraping of metal from the back of the vehicle

POSSIBLE CAUSES
- Muffler has come loose
- Tailpipe has come loose

WHAT TO DO
That scraping sound is probably the muffler or tailpipe being dragged along the road. If you're close to a mechanic's garage, stop off and ask to have the errant piece reattached. (This will take just a moment and shouldn't be expensive.) If the dangling part falls off before you reach a garage, trace back over your travel route to find the missing piece.

If you're not anywhere near a mechanic, pull over to the side of the road in a safe spot where you can get underneath the back end of your car. Give the car a few minutes to cool down, then get down on all fours and peer under the rear end. You ought to be able to see which part is dangling. Wear gloves or use rags to protect your hands from the hot parts. Using rope, elastic cords, duct tape, or whatever you have handy, tie the dangling piece to a nearby bracket — not the driveshaft! — for support. Then bring your car straight to your mechanic.

Strange Sounds from Accessories

The Sound

Squeaking from the air conditioner

POSSIBLE CAUSE
- Normal activity — an air conditioner that has not been used for a while squeaks

WHAT TO DO
Squeaking upon start-up is normal for an air conditioner. Once the unit has been operating for a few minutes, the noise should stop. If any of the components of the air-conditioning unit are actually defective, you'll notice it in the lack of cooling power, not because of squeaking. To keep your car's air-conditioning system in top shape, turn it on for a few minutes every week, regardless of the outside temperature. See page 76 for more details.

The Sound

Buzzing when the windshield wipers are activated

POSSIBLE CAUSES
- Insufficient washer fluid
- Defective windshield wiper motor
- Blown fuse

WHAT TO DO
Are the blades moving? If so, whether or not you have activated the switch to spray windshield washer fluid onto the windshield, the buzzing noise may be telling you that there isn't any windshield washer fluid available. Either the reservoir is empty or the washer fluid in the reservoir is frozen. Pop open the hood and take a look. If the reservoir is empty, fill it — see page 96 for details. If the washer fluid in the reservoir is frozen, drive your car into a heated garage, and keep it there until the washer fluid is liquid again. Once the washer fluid has melted, spray, spray, spray until all the fluid is gone. Before you refill the reservoir, visually inspect it to make sure it hasn't cracked (when liquids freeze, they expand). If there are cracks in the reservoir, go ahead and refill it — with *winter* washer fluid — but call your mechanic and have her order a replacement reservoir for the make and model of your car.

If the wiper blades don't move when you activate them, and their lack of motion is accompanied by a buzzing sound, then either a fuse is blown or the motor that drives the wiper blades is defective. Check and, if necessary, replace the fuse that's linked to the windshield wipers, following the instructions on page 136. If the fuse seems fine, book an appointment with your mechanic at your earliest convenience.

Sleuthing with Your Nose

Ah, the noxious smell of exhaust fumes. When you're stuck behind a big rig, a lumbering truck, or a backfiring clunker of a car, the choking odor is sometimes strong enough to make you want to hold your breath. Even when you roll up the windows, the smell persists, seeping in through the heating and cooling vents. You're helpless to do anything other than wait it out.

But hold on a minute. What if the noxious odor is coming from your car? Better question: How can you tell if the noxious odor is coming from your car, not from some passing vehicle? Most odors that may offend your nose while you're on the road can be symptoms of a serious engine malfunction. But when you're surrounded by other vehicles, it can be difficult to determine if your car is the source of the smell.

Generally speaking, if an odor comes on strong and you don't see a big honkin' source sitting right in front of you — a rusty truck emitting veritable clouds of black exhaust smoke, for example — you should pull over to the side of the road to make sure that your car isn't the source of the smell. Just leave the engine running, step outside the car, and let your nose do the sleuthing. If the odor dissipates, it probably didn't originate in your car. If the odor persists, follow the advice given in the next few pages.

Strange Smells

The Smell

Burning oil when you start up the engine, which then dissipates

POSSIBLE CAUSES
- Low automatic transmission fluid
- Internal engine block leak
- Oil leak around exhaust manifold (evident also by blue or black smoke coming from the exhaust system)

WHAT TO DO

Once you've smelled burning oil, you'll recognize the odor. It's not the same as burning rubber, but it's just as distinct.

Check the automatic transmission fluid, following the instructions on page 62, and top off if necessary. A transmission fluid leak can be a serious problem, so if the automatic transmission fluid runs low more than once, bring the problem to the attention of your mechanic.

If the level of automatic transmission fluid is fine, then you may have a malfunction in the engine block. Bring your car to your mechanic for a complete evaluation as soon as possible.

The Smell

Burning paint

POSSIBLE CAUSE
- Malfunction in cooling system

WHAT TO DO

What does paint have to do with the cooling system? Nothing — but the smell of a cooling system malfunction is strangely similar to the smell of burning paint. Because the cooling system is vital to your car's well-being, book an immediate appointment with your mechanic to have your car checked out.

The Smell

Burning plastic

POSSIBLE CAUSES
- Wire short-circuiting
- Wire insulation burning

WHAT TO DO

A wiring malfunction can emit the odor of burning plastic. You don't want to touch exposed wires or wires that are dispelling heat. Your best course of action is to call your mechanic and get your car into her garage for an immediate evaluation.

Burning rubber

POSSIBLE CAUSES
- Hot tire
- Worn brakes
- Fire inside a tire

WHAT TO DO

If you've ever been near a car peeling away to a furious start, tires screeching against the pavement, then you've probably had a whiff of the smell of burning rubber. The smell comes from hot tires. The heat comes from the friction of rubber against pavement. When you accelerate too quickly from a full stop, the rubber tire squeals as it spins against the pavement, and the friction between the pavement and the tire generates heat. A tire can also become hot if you drive at excessive speeds.

When a tire becomes very hot, it can ignite on the inside, resulting in an internal fire. An explosion could result. If you haven't just made a screeching start and you smell burning rubber, pull over to the side of the road. Approach each tire cautiously, with your hands outstretched and palms out. If you feel heat radiating from any tire, stay away from it and call for a tow truck.

If the tires feel fine but the smell persists as you drive, suspect the brakes. When brakes are excessively worn, they perform miserably, and the tires may slide along the pavement when you brake. That, too, will generate the smell of burning rubber. Immediately take your car to your mechanic for an examination of the brakes on the front and rear wheels.

The Smell

Exhaust fumes

POSSIBLE CAUSES
- Emissions from other vehicles around you
- Faulty exhaust system

WHAT TO DO

Ever been caught in heavy stop-and-go traffic in the heat of mid-summer? Not only is your patience put to the test, but that smell — those exhaust fumes are enough to make you nauseous. Use the air recirculation climate control setting so that as little of the outside exhaust fumes get inside your car. Keep your distance from the vehicle in front of you so that its exhaust fumes dissipate into the air rather than passing through the front grille of your car.

Don't indiscriminately attribute all exhaust fumes to passing vehicles, however. If your exhaust system is malfunctioning, it could be leaking fumes into the passenger compartment of your car. These carbon monoxide fumes are potentially deadly. If you're not sure where the smell is coming from, drive with your windows down to allow fresh air inside the car. If the smell persists, immediately take the car to your mechanic to have the exhaust system checked out. Under no circumstances drive with the windows up. Fresh air, no matter how hot or cold, could keep you alive.

The Smell

Gasoline

POSSIBLE CAUSES
- Faulty fuel-injection system
- Fuel line leak
- Fuel tank leak
- Defective fuel pump
- Gas cap left open

WHAT TO DO
Anytime you smell gasoline, other than just after having left the gas station, stop driving. Sniff your way around your car. If you detect the smell of gasoline coming from your car, play it safe and call a tow truck. A leak in the fuel system could lead to an explosion.

If the gasoline smell dissipates, it may have come from a passing vehicle. If this is the case, you can continue on your way, but if the gasoline smell returns, play it safe: Stop driving and call a tow truck.

The Smell

Oil

POSSIBLE CAUSES
- Low or no engine oil
- Clogged emission control system(s)
- Incorrect engine oil grade
- A passing diesel vehicle
- An oil refinery in the area

WHAT TO DO
Check the oil, following the instructions on page 82, and add more oil if necessary. If the level of engine oil seems adequate, or if you top off the oil and the odor persists, bring the car to your mechanic at your earliest convenience for a checkup. As with most things automotive, it's best to err on the side of caution, instead of taking a chance and ending up with serious mechanical failure. If, for example, one of the emission control systems in your car is clogged, generating the odor of oil, but you do nothing about it and continue driving, the end result will probably be a defective component, which will be expensive to replace.

Of course, before you make the call to your mechanic, stop and think. Are you driving through an area where an oil refinery is located? Did you just pass by a diesel vehicle? Both can emit the odor of oil.

Leaks Inside and Outside the Car

If there are puddles revealed underneath your car when you pull out of a parking spot, or if the carpet under the dashboard feels squishy and damp, you have a fluid leak. In most cases, the leak is happening under the hood, and the fluid is seeping down through the engine to end up under your car or under the dashboard. Also, in most cases, the leak necessitates a mechanic's attention. What you can do is identify the possible causes of the leak and determine whether you need an immediate appointment with your mechanic.

WHAT FLUID IS IT?	
COLOR	**MOST LIKELY CANDIDATE**
Green	Coolant
Pink	Coolant
Clear	Water
Brown	Engine oil
Black	Engine oil
Reddish brown	Automatic transmission or power steering fluid
Light tan	Brake fluid, power steering fluid, or gasoline

Don't be nonchalant about a couple of drops of something on the driveway beneath your car. A slow leak, if left unattended, can quickly lead to a major mechanical problem. And a small leak can usually be repaired easily; if it becomes a big leak, the repair will usually involve much more manpower hours at your mechanic's garage, plus a slew of new components. The result: a hefty repair bill.

Fluid Leaks

The Problem

Water on the pavement under your car

POSSIBLE CAUSE
- Condensation from the air conditioner

WHAT TO DO
This is normal. In fact, if you've been using the air conditioner and there isn't water under the car, the air-conditioning unit may be defective, and it should be examined by your mechanic.

The Problem

Engine oil on the pavement under your car

POSSIBLE CAUSE
- Leak from the oil filter or oil pan

WHAT TO DO
If you've just had your oil changed, march yourself, your car, and your receipt straight back to the garage and ask to have the job redone. It could be that the new oil filter wasn't tightened properly or that the old rubber gasket that sealed the old oil filter in place wasn't removed, and a new rubber gasket was secured on top of it. If the seal between the new oil filter and the shaft of the engine block isn't tight, oil will leak.

It could also be that the bolt that holds the oil pan closed is stripped and, therefore, is not providing a tight seal. Oil could then drip from the pan.

If you haven't just had the oil changed, bring the car to your mechanic at your earliest convenience for a diagnosis.

The Problem

Coolant on the pavement under your car

POSSIBLE CAUSE
- A leak in the cooling system

WHAT TO DO
If the coolant is leaking quickly — enough to deplete the coolant reservoir so that you have to top it off (see page 70) — book an immediate appointment with your mechanic. If the coolant is leaking very slowly, you can take care of it at your earliest convenience. First, however, wipe up the spilled coolant with a rag; it's poisonous, and you don't want any neighborhood cats or dogs licking it up. Place the rag in a plastic bag and dispose of it in a covered garbage container.

The Problem

Automatic transmission fluid on the pavement under your car

POSSIBLE CAUSE
• Leak from the automatic transmission fluid pan or lines

WHAT TO DO
Check the automatic transmission fluid pan, if you can access it, for wet spots. Noticeable moisture could indicate, for example, that the bolt on the pan isn't tight enough, so that a constant drip results. If the pan is sealed and doesn't have a bolt, it could be that the seal is wearing down and allowing fluid to accumulate on the outside. *When* you take the car to the mechanic will depend on how serious the leak is. If the automatic transmission fluid is leaking steadily — enough to deplete the reservoir so that you have to top it off (see page 62) — book an immediate appointment with your mechanic. If it's leaking very slowly, you can take care of the problem at your earliest convenience.

The Problem

Power steering fluid on the pavement under your car

POSSIBLE CAUSE
• Leak from the power steering fluid reservoir or hoses

WHAT TO DO
Check the power steering reservoir for wet streaks of fluid. Where is the moisture? On the reservoir itself or on the hose extending from the reservoir? Relay this information to your mechanic at your earliest convenience.

The Problem

Gasoline on the pavement under your car

POSSIBLE CAUSE
• Leak from the fuel system

WHAT TO DO
If you spot what looks and smells like a gasoline leak, you have a problem that needs to be taken care of right away. Gasoline is highly flammable — you don't want it dripping on hot engine parts under the hood. Immediately take your car to your mechanic for a thorough evaluation.

Fluid Leaks

The Problem

Brake fluid on the pavement under your car

POSSIBLE CAUSES
- Leak from brake fluid master cylinder
- Leak from clutch fluid master cylinder

WHAT TO DO
Check both reservoirs and the hoses that extend from them to determine the source of the leak. If the fluid is leaking fast — enough to deplete the reservoir so that you have to top it off (see pages 61 and 89) — book an immediate appointment with your mechanic. If it's leaking very slowly, you can take care of it at your earliest convenience.

The Problem

Water in the trunk

POSSIBLE CAUSES
- Water leaking into trunk during rainstorms
- Windshield washer fluid leaking into trunk

WHAT TO DO
If your trunk seems damp and musty, the weather stripping that seals it may have cracked. Visually inspect the stripping; if it needs to be repaired, consult with your mechanic.

Do you have a rear windshield wiper? If you tend to park your car on a steep incline, it may be windshield washer fluid, not water, that's seeping into the trunk. Over time, gravity forces the fluid from the rear window washer line into the trunk. This scenario has an easy solution — park on level ground!

MUSTY ODORS

If the carpets inside your car have been damaged by moisture, they may begin to smell musty. In this case, consider having the inside of the car professionally steam cleaned. The high heat of the steam will destroy any mold, eliminating that musty odor. If you know the cause of the moisture damage — for example, a leaky air-conditioning unit or a burst jug of milk — relay this information to the steam cleaning staff.

Water or dampness inside the car

POSSIBLE CAUSES
- Loose or cracked air-conditioning hose
- Leak at the base of the windshield
- Cracked or loose weather stripping around doors

WHAT TO DO

If moisture collects inside your car after a rainfall, the weather stripping around the doors is probably loose or worn. Visually inspect the stripping; if it needs to be repaired, consult with your mechanic.

If the moisture collects inside your car after a snowfall, it could be that you've damaged the grille just below the front windshield while hacking and scraping away at ice. If this is the case, you'll need an auto body shop, not a mechanic — but perhaps your mechanic can recommend a good shop to you.

If your car has air-conditioning and you notice moisture accumulating under the dashboard, have your mechanic inspect the air-conditioning system. Book the appointment as soon as possible — the refrigerant inside the air-conditioning system is highly combustible, and you certainly don't want a puddle of it sitting around inside your car, nor do you want it spattering on hot engine components under the hood.

Coolant under the dashboard

POSSIBLE CAUSES
- Faulty heater core
- Cracked heater hose or valve

WHAT TO DO

If you notice a greenish or pink puddle on the floor under the dashboard, the heater core, hose, or valve is probably malfunctioning. Have your mechanic take a look at these components and repair or replace them as necessary. Coolant is toxic, and the fumes it emits can give you a headache, so this is a problem you should have taken care of as soon as possible.

Steering, Stalling, and Suspension

Sometimes the best of intentions to keep your car mechanically sound will not keep it 100 percent healthy. Maintenance is key and will go a long way toward preventing automotive woe and misfortune, but it's not foolproof. Components wear out. Systems malfunction. Usually at inopportune moments. You can prevent a lot of problems, but not all of them.

The following pages outline some of the most common "handling" dysfunctions that drivers encounter. These include some rather subtle problems, such as your car seeming to pull in one direction and feeling like it vibrates more than is normal. You want to stay alert to such symptoms, but you also don't want to become paranoid. Cars are generally quite sturdy, and they can handle quite a bit of abuse before they begin to show signs of wear and tear.

So stay alert and be cautious, but most of all, use your common sense. The tips that follow should be of assistance in determining the gravity of a range of handling problems.

Steering, Stalling, and Suspension

The Problem

The car gives a jolting ride, rather than a smooth one

POSSIBLE CAUSE
- Defective shock absorber

WHAT TO DO
When the shocks begin to deteriorate, it's wise to speak with your mechanic, who can offer advice on how serious the problem is. You don't have to replace the shocks just because they're not working perfectly. Your car can bounce all it wants and you'll still be able to drive it. The question is: How much tolerance do you have for a jolting, jarring ride?

When you reach the limit of your tolerance, bring your car to your mechanic to have the shocks replaced.

The Problem

The engine runs fine, but the car does not move when you depress the gas pedal

POSSIBLE CAUSES
- Objects blocking tires
- Sticking brake pads
- Low or dirty automatic transmission fluid
- Slipping clutch disc
- Misadjusted clutch

WHAT TO DO
Hop out of your car and take a quick walk around it to make sure that no objects are lodged in front of or behind the wheels. If the wheels are clear, pop open the hood and check the automatic transmission fluid (if your car has an automatic transmission). Top off if necessary (see page 62 for instructions).

If the transmission fluid seems fine, or if topping off the fluid doesn't get your car moving, your brake pads may be sticking. If you've recently driven your car through deep water or if there's been a rainstorm, the brakes can become waterlogged, which makes them stick, so that the tires won't move. If this is the case, you'll have to wait for them to dry out before you'll be able to get going. (You can take the tires off the car to speed up the process, if you like.)

If none of these tips gets your car moving, call a tow truck and have the car towed to your mechanic's garage.

Steering, Stalling, and Suspension

The Problem

Car has no power or loses power when accelerating

POSSIBLE CAUSES

- Low fuel
- Battery charge is low
- Dirty or loose battery cables
- Damp or cracked distributor cap
- Frayed or loose spark plug wire(s)
- Incorrectly gapped or dirty spark plug(s)
- Slipping clutch
- Defective computer system
- Clogged emission control system
- Clogged fuel filter
- Blocked or leaking fuel line
- Defective fuel pump
- Leaking head gasket
- Clogged or defective catalytic converter
- Bent or clogged muffler or tailpipe
- Worn-out pistons

WHAT TO DO

Check the gas gauge. Are you running low on fuel? If so, stop worrying about mechanical problems and make a commitment to keep the tank at least half full at all times. For now, find a service station and fill 'er up.

Most of the possible reasons why your car would lose power while accelerating are indicators of a serious mechanical problem that will require the attention of your mechanic. There are, however, a few possibilities you can investigate and address on your own. First, open the hood and look at the battery. Are the battery cables loose? Are the cable ends frayed? If necessary, tighten the cables, even if the ends are frayed — but if the ends *are* frayed, have the battery cables changed as soon as possible. Check the amount of electrolyte in each of the battery cells. If any of the cells are running low on electrolyte, add distilled water. If the battery posts and battery cables are caked with white acid buildup, clean them. (See pages 48–51 for details on refilling and cleaning batteries.)

If your car has a distributor cap, remove it and visually inspect the outside and inside of the cap, checking for cracks. (See page 206 for details.) If it is cracked, ask your mechanic to order a new one for you.

Make sure all the spark plug wires are attached to their respective spark plugs. (Wear rubber gloves so you don't get a shock.) If the wires are frayed at their ends, have your mechanic replace them.

If your investigation has not yielded the cause of the problem, it's time to enlist the help of your mechanic. Make an appointment as soon as possible.

The Problem

Car pulls to one side when accelerating

POSSIBLE CAUSES
- Front tire on the side the car is pulling toward is flat or has low air pressure
- Uneven tread on a front tire
- Different-sized front tires
- Wheels are out of alignment
- Loose or defective rack-and-pinion steering unit
- Defective shock absorber(s)
- Broken or sagging springs
- Worn-out ball joints

WHAT TO DO
Pull over to a safe spot and take a look at your front tires. If one is flat, change it (see page 200 for instructions). Check the air pressure in both front tires; if one has low air pressure, add more air as soon as possible (see page 112 for details.) Examine the tread on both tires; if one tire's tread is worn or irregular (see pages 110–111 for diagrams), bring the problem to the attention of your mechanic.

If you can't identify the cause of the problem, book an appointment with your mechanic as soon as possible. The front wheels may need to be aligned, or there could be a problem with the suspension system. Your mechanic will be able to diagnose and resolve these problems.

The Problem

Car stalls in cold weather

POSSIBLE CAUSES
- Dirty air filter
- Battery charge is low
- Defective coolant temperature sensor
- Dirty fuel injectors
- Clogged fuel filter
- Defective fuel pump
- Faulty spark plug

WHAT TO DO
You can check the air filter and battery yourself (see pages 40 and 44, respectively), but if it's cold enough to make your teeth chatter and you can get your car started, even temporarily, you might be better off driving straight to your mechanic's garage. It will be warm there, and your mechanic can replace an air filter or recharge or replace a battery in no time at all. And if the cause of the problem happens not to be the air filter or battery, then the car is already at the garage, where your mechanic can give it a thorough examination.

The Problem

Car stalls in hot weather

POSSIBLE CAUSES
- Defective cooling system components
- Vapor lock in fuel line

WHAT TO DO
See page 210 for tips on what to do when your car overheats.

EARLY ACTION

A car that idles roughly or that tends to stall should be examined by a mechanic. These are small problems that probably won't prevent you from driving, but if left unattended, a more complex — and expensive — mechanical problem may develop.

The Problem

Car stalls when the engine is idling

POSSIBLE CAUSES
- Bad or low gas in fuel tank
- Dirty air filter
- Low automatic transmission fluid
- Clogged fuel filter
- Faulty spark plug(s)
- Defective thermostat

WHAT TO DO
Fill up the gas tank if you need to. If you've just filled up and now the car is stalling when the engine idles, you may have gotten a tank of bad gas. Pour a bottle of fuel additive into the tank, following the instructions on the product label. Refuel the car, even if it's only a couple of dollars' worth of gas, just to get good gas into the fuel system.

If gas is not the problem, check the air filter. If it's dirty or overdue for replacement, install a new filter. (See page 40 for advice.) Check the automatic transmission fluid, following the instructions on page 62.

If none of the above solves the problem, book an appointment with your mechanic at your earliest convenience.

The Problem

Car moves when the parking brake is engaged

POSSIBLE CAUSE
- Loose or broken parking brake cable

WHAT TO DO
The parking brake cable connects to the brakes on the rear wheels. If it is working properly, your car shouldn't move when the parking brake is engaged, even if you forget

to disengage it before starting up the engine and pressing down on the gas pedal.

If the parking brake doesn't secure your car in place when activated, the parking brake cable may be loose or broken. Have your mechanic tighten or replace the cable at your earliest convenience. In the meantime, don't engage the parking brake.

The Problem

Car is difficult to steer

POSSIBLE CAUSES
- Flat tire
- Low or uneven tire pressure
- Front wheels out of alignment
- Low power steering fluid
- Loose or broken belt on power steering pump
- Defective power steering pump
- Worn-out ball joints

- Hose at power steering pump is loose, broken, or kinked
- Damaged front-end suspension components
- Worn-out rack-and-pinion steering unit
- Dry, cracked rubber seals at ends of rack-and-pinion steering unit

WHAT TO DO
Steering difficulties are caused by defective steering components, tire problems, or worn-out suspension components. You can easily check the tires. If one is flat, change it, following the instructions on page 200. Check the air pressure in each tire and add more air if necessary, following the instructions on page 112. If the tires don't seem to be the problem, make an appointment with your mechanic to have the steering and suspension systems checked out.

The Problem

Car vibrates or shakes when moving

POSSIBLE CAUSES
- Incorrect tire pressure on one front tire
- Loose lug nuts at the wheel
- Unbalanced front tires
- Defective CV- or U-joint
- Worn-out driveshaft
- Defective fuel injectors
- Loose exhaust pipe
- Defective shock absorber
- Incorrectly gapped spark plug
- Worn-out steering linkage
- Defective brakes
- Air locked inside brake system

WHAT TO DO
It can be scary to have the steering wheel start shaking in your hands. The first thing to do is to check the air pressure in each of the tires,

adding or releasing air as necessary. (See page 112 for details.) Also check the lug nuts, making sure that they're secured tightly.

The shaking may be caused by tires that are unbalanced. If the shaking is noticeable at highway speeds, it's the front tires that are unbalanced. If the shaking is intermittent, it's probably the rear tires that are unbalanced. Regardless of the circumstances, make an appointment with your mechanic at your earliest convenience to have the problem diagnosed and resolved. If the cause of the problem is something other than unbalanced wheels, it could be progressive — the longer you wait, the more expensive the repair becomes, and the more dangerous the problem becomes for you and your passengers.

The Problem

Car weaves back and forth

POSSIBLE CAUSES
- Flat rear tire
- Worn-out suspension components
- Wheels are out of alignment

WHAT TO DO
Pull over to the roadside and check for a flat tire. (See page 200 for instructions on changing a flat tire.)

If a flat tire isn't the problem, it may be that the wheels are out of alignment or suspension components have worn out to the point that they can't properly do their job. Get your car into your mechanic's garage as soon as possible to avoid further mechanical problems.

ON THE ROAD

If a steering problem suddenly occurs while you're on the road, place both hands firmly on the steering wheel at the 4 o'clock and 8 o'clock positions. This is the safest position for your hands; in the event that the air bag deploys, you're at a lesser risk for breaking fingers or wrists. Ease up on the accelerator and keep you eyes focused on the task at hand — getting your car safely to the side of the road.

Lights and Blinkers

It's easy to notice when your headlights aren't working — driving around in the dark is not an easy task, not to mention that it's illegal. But if the headlights were dimmer than they should be, you might not notice, or you might suspect your eyesight. And how would you ever know if the brake or turn signal lights at the rear of your car weren't working?

Headlights are, of course, intended to help you see after dark. Equally important, they let other drivers know that you're on the road. Turn signal lights and brake lights let other drivers know what your intentions are. Isn't is annoying when the driver in front of you makes a sudden turn without using her turn signal? You can appreciate, then, that the driver behind you would look for the same courtesy. When your bulbs are dim or malfunctioning, this vital communication is lost.

It's wise to check your front and rear lights periodically to make sure that they work properly. Enlist the help of a friend or family member to look at them for you as you turn on and off the headlights (on low and high beam), press the brake pedal, put the car into reverse, and use the turn signals. The tips on the pages that follow will help you figure out what to do in the event that you uncover a problem.

Lights and Blinkers

The Problem

An exterior light does not function

POSSIBLE CAUSES
- Burned-out bulb
- Defective switch
- Blown fuse
- Loose wiring

AUTOSTUDENT

If you're hesitant to tackle the job of replacing a bulb in your car, bring the car to your mechanic and have her do it for you. Ask to watch while she does the work, so that the next time a bulb in your car burns out, you can handle the task yourself.

WHAT TO DO

If just one of a pair of lights — one of the headlights or brake lights, for example — doesn't work, the most likely culprit is a burned-out bulb. It's not difficult to change a bulb; you can find a replacement bulb in any auto parts store, and your owner's manual will give you instructions for installing it. Follow those instructions carefully, particularly if they require that you dismantle the entire light assembly unit. (Take a Polaroid of the unit before you dismantle it as a visual reminder of how everything should look once you put it back together.)

If the cause of the problem is not a burned-out bulb, check to see if a fuse has blown (see page 137 for details).

If the appropriate fuse doesn't seem to be blown, you've reached the end of do-it-yourself options for the non-mechanically inclined. Bring your car to your mechanic as soon as possible for an evaluation.

The Problem

A headlight works on high beam but not on low beam

POSSIBLE CAUSE
- Burned-out bulb

WHAT TO DO

Purchase a replacement bulb from an auto parts store and follow the instructions in your owner's manual for installing it.

One or both headlights always looks dim

POSSIBLE CAUSES
- Battery charge is low
- Bad wiring
- Worn-out alternator
- Loose alternator belt
- Faulty electrical ground

WHAT TO DO
A headlight that's dim isn't receiving adequate electrical current. It's dangerous to drive with dim headlights — the problem being not that you can't see but that other drivers can't see you — so this is a problem you should take care of immediately.

Pop open the hood and take a good look at the battery. Does each of the battery cells have sufficient electrolyte? If any of the cells are running low, add distilled water. If the battery posts and battery cables are caked with white acid buildup, clean them using a solution of baking soda and water. (See pages 48–51 for details on refilling and cleaning batteries.)

If the battery seems to be fine, bring the car to your mechanic for an evaluation of the wiring and alternator.

A signal light continues blinking after you have completed a turn

POSSIBLE CAUSE
- Defective turn signal switch

WHAT TO DO
The turn signal switch distributes electrical current to the right or left turn signal, depending on which signal you've activated. It's supposed to shut off once the turn is made. If the blinkers keep flashing after you've completed a turn, the switch is probably broken. Call your mechanic and explain the problem; she'll order a new switch for your car and, when it arrives, install it.

ON-THE-ROAD EMERGENCIES

ce storm? Flat tire? Car won't start? Stranded? On-the-road emergencies can inspire true panic if you don't know what to do about them. This section will help you think through the proper course of action for a broad range of emergency situations, both common and uncommon. When you've already mapped out in your head the proper steps for dealing with an emergency, you're more likely to act calmly and quickly in the event that you find yourself in that particular situation.

It's not a bad idea to invest in a cell phone for your car. A cell phone makes it easy to call for help from the road. However, having a cell phone won't make you invincible. Cell phones don't work in many rural locations, and if your phone's battery power has run low, no amount of dialing will bring help. And let's not forget the cost. Some cell phone packages can be quite expensive.

You don't need a cell phone to survive on the road, nor can you rely on a cell phone to get you out of trouble. What you do need is common sense, confidence, and caution. Don't endanger the health of your car by continuing to drive it despite an obvious malfunction. Don't endanger your own safety by allowing impatience to guide your decision making, by abandoning your car or by hitching a ride with a stranger.

Above all, be prepared. Practice removing a tire and putting it back on in the comfort of your driveway at home, so that when you need to change a flat tire on the side of the road, you have previous experience to call upon. Read through chapter 2 and familiarize yourself with the vital innards of your car's engine, so that when strange noises or odd smells start coming from the engine, you'll know what to do. Prepare a tool kit and an emergency kit for your car, and stow them in waterproof containers in the trunk. With a little preparation, good information, and the proper tools, you'll be equipped to handle any car emergency.

Getting Prepared

Being prepared for emergencies entails more than knowing how to change a flat tire or what to do when your brakes fail. You also need to carry with you the tools and supplies that help you evaluate what's wrong with your car, fix mechanical problems, and stay safe in those times that you must wait for help.

The following car-prep checklists outline all the supplies you might need to handle just about any automobiling emergency. The tool kit contains equipment for quick on-the-road repairs; the emergency kit contains food, water, and extra clothing in the event that you find yourself stranded in the middle of nowhere.

Purchase a large plastic bin with a lid for each kit. Bundle the supplies inside the bins and stow them in the trunk of your car.

In addition to preparing these kits, keep a tire pressure gauge, a tread depth gauge, and a second flashlight in your glove compartment, along with your owner's manual, so that they'll be right at hand when you need them.

AUTOTALK

Keep a small fire extinguisher under one of the front seats, where it will be handy if a fire starts under the hood or inside a tire.

You might also consider installing a small, battery-operated carbon monoxide detector underneath a front seat or under the dashboard. If your exhaust system becomes defective and begins leaking carbon monoxide fumes into the passenger compartment, the detector will sound. Replace the batteries every six months.

Automotive Tool Kit

Make sure that the fluids — engine oil, brake fluid, and so on — are the types recommended for your car; check your owner's manual for details.

- Automatic transmission fluid (if your car is an automatic)
- Brake fluid (small unopened can)
- Engine oil
- Fuel additive
- Nonvolatile emergency fuel
- Power steering fluid (small unopened can)
- Premixed coolant (see page 71 to learn how to mix coolant)
- Stop-leak additive for the cooling system
- Tire sealant
- WD-40
- Windshield washer fluid
- Funnel
- Empty gas container
- Booster (jumper) cables, 16 feet (5 m), 16-gauge with sturdy clamps

- Air filter (the right size and type for your car)
- Rubber or plastic gloves
- Flathead and Phillips head screwdrivers
- Four-armed wheel (lug) wrench
- Hammer
- Jack and jack stand
- Six wood blocks (for securing tires in place when you're changing a flat)
- Warning reflectors or emergency flares
- Clean rags or paper towels
- Small bottle of soda water (for removing stains)
- Rope or towing chain
- Aluminum foil (to place over a fuel line to cure vapor lock — see page 214)
- Reflective tape (to place over a broken head- or taillight)
- Duct tape (because you never know when it might come in handy)
- Oversized, bright-colored shirt (for when you must work on your car)

Emergency Kit

It may seem extreme to be stockpiling extra clothing, food, and water in your car, but should you ever need that extra sweater, a dry match, a drink of water, or other emergency supplies, it will be a relief to know that help is in the trunk of your car. Replace the food and water every spring and fall.

- Backpack (to carry supplies if you decide to leave your car)
- Wool blanket or sleeping bag
- Candles and an empty tin for holding a lit candle
- Waterproof matches or a cigarette lighter
- Loose change to make a phone call (even if you have a cellular phone; it might not work everywhere you travel)
- White or bright-colored cloth (to tie to the radio antenna or door handle as a distress signal)
- First-aid kit
- Small flashlight (with the batteries removed)
- Transistor radio (with the batteries removed)
- Batteries for the flashlight and transistor radio (they'll last longer when removed from the radio and flashlight)
- Nonperishable food items, such as candies, crackers, jam, and trail mix
- Drinking water
- Extra set of car keys, including keys to the doors and the trunk
- Shovel and ax (you can find compact, collapsible shovels and axes at most hardware and camping supply stores)
- Diapers, canned milk, extra clothing, and toys or activity books for infants and children, if you regularly travel with them
- Personal clothing appropriate to the climate
- Reading material and a deck of cards (to pass the time if you're stuck in the middle of nowhere)
- Outdoor survival kit, which includes a compass, miniature flashlight, pocketknife, compact plastic raincoat, a bag of high-energy trail mix, a small bottle of drinking water, waterproof matches, and a whistle

Winterizing

Ice, snow, sleet, and frigid temperatures during the winter months wouldn't be so difficult to handle if we could all stay warm and snug indoors by the fire and venture outside only when we wanted to. Unfortunately, in our busy lives, we often have no time to wait for weather to clear, roads to be plowed and sanded, or temperatures to rise. If you live in a city, town, or rural location that experiences annual snowfall, add the following to the tool kit in the trunk of your car before winter begins:

- Kitty litter, newspaper, carpet remnants, a bag of salt, or a traction mat (to provide traction under the tires)
- Lock de-icer
- Gas-line antifreeze
- Snow brush with an attached ice scraper

With these few items and your emergency kit — which you've updated for the winter by adding extra warm clothing and boots, right? — you should now be equipped to survive yet another season of snow and plummeting temperatures.

AUTOTALK

Gasoline is formulated to prevent freezing. But in severe cold — when temperatures drop below 0°F (-18°C) — adding gas-line antifreeze to the fuel tank can prevent start-up trouble. Just follow the instructions on the product label.

To keep the locks on your car doors and trunk from freezing, every year before winter sets in, lightly coat your car door key with WD-40 and insert it into each of the locks. The lubrication provides a barrier against the buildup of moisture.

Using a Block Heater

If you live in a climate where temperatures become downright frigid during the long winter nights, you probably already know a great deal about block heaters. For the uninitiated, however, here's a quick explanation.

When temperatures plunge far below freezing, your engine becomes too cold to start up. Vital engine fluids become thick, components start to stick to each other, the starter motor becomes very sluggish, and the battery becomes practically comatose.

A block heater keeps your engine warm so that it will start up readily even in sub-zero temperatures. The block heater is installed under the hood, near the engine block. It has an electrical three-prong plug, which can be found under the hood or extending through the car's front grille. You use a sturdy electrical extension cord to connect the block heater's plug to a nearby GFCI-protected electrical outlet. (Connect the extension cord to the block heater first and the GFCI outlet second; you don't want to have electrical current flowing while you're reaching around with the end of the extension cord trying to find the block heater plug.) Electrical current from your house or garage keeps the engine block warm and cozy so that, in the cold and dark morning, the battery and starter don't have to work so hard to get electrical juices flowing, and you can get on the road.

Before the colder months set in, check that the block heater is working properly. Plug it in, and within a couple of minutes you should hear a sizzling sound.

One of the most common mistakes car owners make is to plug in the block heater all night, every night, throughout the winter months. Research shows that you really need to use the block heater only when the temperature is predicted to drop below 5°F (-15° C). And you don't need to keep it running all night; that's a waste of electricity. Instead, plug it in two to four hours before you need your car. If you don't want to wake up in the wee hours of the morning to plug in the block heater, invest in an outdoor timer that will switch on the power at the appropriate hour.

Staying in Control

There is no on-the-road emergency like being behind the wheel but not in control of your car. In a situation like this, you don't have time to carefully plot out your course of action and put the plan into action. You have to make a split-second decision. For that decision to be the best possible one, you must already have thought through and mapped out the proper reactions to skidding, hydroplaning, brake failure, and so on. If you practice visualizing yourself taking the necessary steps to correct an out-of-control car, you're more likely to stay calm and act quickly to correct the problem when it occurs.

Skidding

Not even the best driver can avoid slipping and sliding on the road. Ice, wet pavement, oil on the road — sometimes you just can't see that you're about to drive over a slippery surface. Knowing that you *will*, at some point, have a skidding "incident," take some time to familiarize yourself with the best course of action.

When you start to skid, it's important *not* to slam on the brakes. Your first and strongest instinct will be to brake, but instead you should first ease up on the accelerator. With both hands, turn the steering wheel in the direction you want the front of your car to head toward. As soon as the front tires regain traction, the front of your car will start to turn in that direction. Once your car's front bumper is aiming in a straight line toward your target, turn the steering wheel back to center, but watch for skidding in the opposite direction, and correct its direction in the same manner. This happens fast, so you need quick reflexes. It usually takes more than one correction to pull a car out of a skid, so don't panic if you aren't on your way with one turn of the steering wheel.

Hydroplaning

When it's raining heavily or there is standing water on the road, your car's tires may lose contact with the pavement. Your car now glides on the road, with millions of droplets of water acting as a shield between the tires and the pavement. This is called hydroplaning, and it's not a good situation.

You can feel when your car is hydroplaning by the way it handles. The steering wheel suddenly feels loose, and you may even skid. When you feel that you are hydroplaning, or you are concerned that you might hydroplane, slow down. Keep your foot off the brake pedal. Steer straight ahead, and continue driving at a reduced speed. If the rain becomes so intense that it's difficult to see, pull off the road at the next rest stop, diner, or service station. If you have to pull over onto the side of the road, activate the hazard lights so that other drivers will be able to see that you're there.

As a preventive measure, make sure you have four good tires on your car. Deep treads allow water droplets to escape from between a tire and the pavement. Worn treads trap water between a tire and the pavement.

Drifting to the Soft Shoulder

Highways are built with soft shoulders for a couple of reasons: to alert drivers when they have driven off the main part of the road and to save money (soft-shoulder materials don't cost as much as the hard-paved surfaces of highways). If you drift onto the soft shoulder at highway speed, it's easy to lose control of your car if you don't take the proper steps.

Most important, do not attempt to swerve your car right back onto the paved road. Also, don't brake hard — you'll send your car into a skid if you do. Instead, keep a firm grip on the steering wheel (two hands, please), ease up on the gas pedal, then gently apply pressure to the brake pedal. You're not going to brake to a full stop; you just want to slow down enough that you can establish control over your car.

When you feel that you have the car under control, ease it back carefully onto the main road (first checking, of course, for oncoming traffic).

Stopping Suddenly

Stop reading right now. Go out to your car and get your owner's manual. Look in the index under BRAKES. Turn to the correct section and find out whether you have antilock brakes.

Why is it important to know what kind of brakes you have? Conventional wisdom says that to stop suddenly you need to pump the brakes —

that is, put pressure on the brake pedal, then ease up, then apply pressure, then ease up, and so on. This advice works fine for conventional brakes. However, these days most cars are equipped with an antilock braking system (ABS), which does the work of pumping the brakes for you. If you pump the brakes, you'll actually nullify the ABS mechanism.

To stop suddenly in a car equipped with antilock brakes, maintain a steady grip on the steering wheel (using both hands, of course) and apply firm and steady pressure to the brake pedal. This may take a bit of getting used to, but once you've become accustomed to stopping suddenly in this manner, it will become second nature.

Brake Failure

If the braking system in your car develops a leak and loses a great deal of hydraulic fluid, or if that fluid is contaminated, your brakes may fail entirely — you press down on the brake pedal, it sinks to the floor, but nothing happens.

What do you do? First, take a deep breath and stay calm; don't let that adrenaline rush unbalance you. Keep both hands on the steering wheel and your foot away from the gas pedal. Now just do your best to steer away from potential collisions. Pump the parking brake lever as you go. If this doesn't stop your car, shift to a lower gear (in a car with an automatic transmission, this means shifting from *D* to *2* and then *1*). Shifting down while the car is moving fast could damage the parking brake and the transmission system, but under the circumstances, you don't have many other choices.

I'm Stuck!

If your car is spinning its wheels in a snowdrift or mud puddle, don't panic. First, stop revving the engine before it overheats or the tires start developing bald spots. Next, roll down your window so that you can hear which tires are spinning. When you've identified which tires are stuck, put something under them for traction, such as kitty litter or old carpets. Get back in the driver's seat, take a deep breath, and try rocking your car.

How do you rock a car? Your stuck tires are most likely in a bit of a rut. Shift into *D* (or first gear in a standard), touch the accelerator, and roll the tires up one side of the rut. Before you get to the top — and before the tires start spinning again — shift to *R* (or reverse in a standard), let your car roll back to the bottom of the rut, touch the accelerator, and bring the tires up the other side of the rut. That's one rock. Repeat, rocking the tires back and forth in the rut, using the car's momentum to bring the tires a little closer to the top of the rut each time. After a few rocks, you should be able to pull your tires out of the rut.

Once your car is unstuck, check the tires for bald spots. If you see any, get replacement tires as soon as possible. And because the engine has been working overtime, wait a few minutes before driving off to give it a chance to cool down.

AUTOTALK

If you're having trouble getting out of an icy or muddy spot, release some air from the tires. This brings more of the tire tread in contact with the ground, which may give you the traction you need to get your car moving. Remove the cap from the valve stem and use the tire pressure gauge to release a small amount of air from the tire (see page 113). Afterward, as soon as you can, reinflate the tire(s) to the recommended pressure.

If You Run Out of Gas

It happens to even the best of us at least once. Some of us would shamefacedly admit that we've done it more than once. Running out of gas seems like a silly thing to do, but it happens, so it's best to be prepared. Purchase a container of emergency fuel additive and stow it in the tool kit that you keep in the trunk of your car. Unlike gasoline, it's nonvolatile, so it's safe to keep in your car.

In the event that you run out of gas, a bottle of emergency fuel will carry the car 10 to 15 miles (16–25 km) — and that, let's hope, is far enough to get you to a gas station. Just pour the contents of the bottle into the fuel tank, following the instructions on the product label. Keep in mind that most types of emergency fuel additive will work only when the engine is warm. If you run out of gas, pour the emergency fuel into the gas tank immediately, without letting the engine cool down.

If you don't have emergency fuel additive in your tool kit and you're near a gas station, get out your empty gasoline container and start hiking.

However, if you're not near a gas station, stay with the car. Consult What to Do When You're Stranded on page 219 for advice on getting help. If a helpful stranger stops to offer you a lift to a gas station, decline politely, and ask instead that he or she take your gasoline container and your spare change, fill up the container, and return it to you.

Changing a Flat Tire

Flat tires are one of the most common automotive problems we encounter on the road. Should one of the tires blow out while you're driving, the car may jerk and suddenly become difficult to maneuver. However, it's not difficult to regain control. The most important thing is not to panic. Hold the steering wheel firmly with both hands, keep driving your car in a straight line, slowly take your foot off the gas pedal, and gently put your foot on the brake pedal. Steer yourself toward the side of the road and slowly ease to a stop, as far from traffic as possible.

It should take only 10 to 15 minutes to change a flat tire, given that you have all the necessary tools and know how to use them. (You've already practiced how to change a tire in the safe confines of your driveway, right?) But before you make the decision to change the flat tire right then and there, carefully examine your situation. If you are parked in a location where traffic is heavy or where you and your car are difficult for oncoming traffic to see, forfeit changing the tire yourself and get help. Most highways and byways are well traveled by law enforcement officers. When they see your car stranded on the side of the road, they'll stop to see what the problem is. If you haven't already called for a tow truck, they can place the call for you.

If you're in a sticky traffic situation, remember also that, as long as you go very slowly, you can drive on a flat tire. Just put on your flashers, stick to the right-hand lane or the shoulder of the road, and drive slowly to the nearest gas station or service center, where the staff can change the tire for you or call a tow truck. Sure, you'll ruin the tire and tire rim, but you'll be safe. The tire and rim can be replaced; you can't.

Step-by-step instructions for changing a flat tire begin on page 200.

Using Tire Sealant

Tire sealant is pressurized foam that you can inject into a flat tire to fill and seal it. At best, tire sealant is a temporary solution; it won't last, and you should have the tire repaired or replaced immediately — at the next service station that you pass. Many mechanics don't like repairing tires that have sealant in them. Why? The sealant smells terrible, and it's a messy job to get it out from inside the tire. If you find yourself in a situation where you have a flat tire but aren't able to change it, go ahead and use tire sealant. But be prepared to purchase a new tire when you get to the nearest garage.

Driving with a Spare Tire

A compact spare tire is smaller than a regular tire, and it's not meant to be used like a regular tire. With a compact spare tire on one of your car's wheels, never drive faster than 50 mph (80 kph) or whatever maximum speed is indicated on the sidewall of the spare tire. It is also not recommended that you drive more than 60 miles (100 km) with a spare tire. Think of the spare tire as a temporary solution to be used in an emergency situation only. Get the flat tire repaired or replaced as soon as possible, and reinstall it on your car. Check that the spare hasn't been damaged, and then return it to its appropriate position in the trunk.

CAUTION

As you approach a flat tire, hold out the back of a hand to it. Does the tire seem to be radiating heat? If a tire seems very hot, a fire may be blazing inside it. While it is hard to determine how hot is too hot, it is best to err on the side of caution and stay away from a hot tire. If it's not on fire, it will soon cool down, and then you can go ahead and change it.

If a tire seem very hot and you suspect that it's on fire, grab the fire extinguisher from under the front seat of your car. If a fire develops, use the fire extinguisher to put out the blaze. Otherwise, stay away from the tire and seek help immediately.

How to Change a Flat

Once you've made the decision to change the flat tire, activate your hazard lights so that oncoming traffic will recognize that your car is disabled. Then follow this simple procedure.

TOOLS & SUPPLIES

- Spare tire
- Three reflectors or flares
- Six pieces of wood or sizable stones
- Flathead screwdriver
- Lug wrench
- Car jack
- Small rag
- Hammer

1 Gather your tools. Remove the spare tire and all other necessary tools and supplies from the trunk of your car. Place them on the ground beside the flat tire.

2 Set out warnings. Set out at least three reflectors or flares. Place one about ten car-lengths behind your car. Place the other reflectors or flares between that flare and your car.

If you do not have reflectors or flares, prop open the hood of your car and tie a bright-colored cloth to the antenna or a traffic-side door handle.

3 Secure the three tires that are not flat by wedging a block of wood or a rock in front of and behind each wheel.

EASY LIFT

Some spare tires aren't compact — they're full-sized tires, and they can be heavy to lift. If you have trouble getting a full-sized spare tire out of the trunk, you might have to get inside the trunk to lift the tire up and over the back wall of the trunk. First remove all items from the trunk (place them well off to the side of the road), which gives you ample room to maneuver inside the trunk. Watch your back so that you don't strain it; bend at the knees when lifting.

4 **Remove the hubcap.** Using a flathead screwdriver, pry loose the hubcap of the flat tire. Place it upside down near you.

5 **Loosen the lug nuts.** Using the lug wrench, loosen the wheel lug nuts by turning them counterclockwise. Move from one lug nut to the other in a crisscross pattern (see the box on page 203). You'll need to apply some

real muscle to this task. Do not fully remove the lug nuts; just get them loose enough that you can remove them by hand once your car has been jacked up.

6 **Position the jack.** Position the jack under the car, following the instructions in your owner's manual.

Most cars have a small notch under their frame that

marks the spot where the jack should be positioned. Place the jack exactly as directed. The jack will hold the tremendous weight of your car; if it is not properly positioned, or if the point of contact where the jack supports the car is not the reinforced position created by the car's manufacturer, damage to your car could result or the jack could give way.

continued on page 202

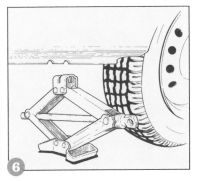

⑦ Jack up the car. Using solid, even strokes on the jack, raise your car until the flat tire is suspended. Keeping your feet away from the car, wiggle the jack and its stand to make sure that it and your car are secure. Walk around your car and double-check the wood blocks or rocks. They should be firmly secured against the other three tires.

⑧ Remove the wheel lug nuts. Remove the lug nuts by hand in a crisscross pattern. Set the lugs in the upside-down hubcap.

⑨ Remove the flat tire. Crouch or sit so that your chest is even with the sidewall of the tire. Using both hands, wiggle the tire loose from the bolts. Roll the tire to the rear of your car.

⑩ Install the spare tire. Roll the spare tire into position. Lift it up, align its notches with the bolts on the wheel rim, and wedge it into place.

⑪ Replace the lug nuts. Replace each lug nut, hand-tightening them clockwise and in a crisscross pattern. When all the lugs are hand-tightened, grab the lug

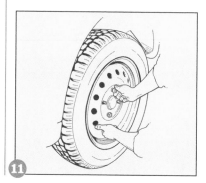

wrench and tighten them further, using the same crisscross pattern. When the tire starts to rotate, you've tightened the lug nuts as much as you should.

⑫ **Lower the car.** Using solid, even strokes, lower the jack until all four tires are flat on the ground. Remove the jack stand from beneath your car.

⑬ **Tighten the lug nuts.** Using the lug wrench, tighten the lug nuts as much as you can, using the crisscross pattern. If the lugs aren't tight, the tire will wobble. If you don't think you have the muscle for it, do your best now, but stop at the next service station and have one of the mechanics tighten the lug nuts with a hydraulic wrench.

⑭ **Replace the hubcap.** Hold the hubcap in place with one hand in the middle and tap around the outside of the hubcap with a rag-covered hammer. Don't pound too hard; you might dent the hubcap.

⑮ **Clean up.** Set the flat tire and all the tools and supplies back inside the trunk.

CRISSCROSS

When you tighten a lug nut, you pull the wheel in that direction. If the next lug nut you tighten is adjacent to the first lug nut, you may inadvertently introduce a slight tilt to the wheel position; it won't straighten out when you tighten the remaining lug nuts. To prevent this, tighten lug nuts in a crisscross pattern, as shown.

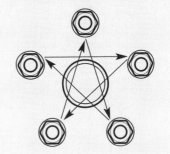

When Your Car Won't Start

You settle into the driver's seat, pull the car door closed, and insert the ignition key to start 'er up. This time, though, there isn't any "up." The engine turns over but it doesn't catch. Or perhaps it sounds like it has a wracking cough but it won't engage. Maybe it just clicks. Or perhaps there's just dead silence — no *vrooom-vrooom*, no clicking, no engine turning, no nothing. Argh!

Step 1: Check the Battery

There are many reasons why your car will not start, but the most common culprit is the battery. Perhaps you left on an electrical accessory — the headlights seem to be the most popular — when you parked your car. (For an overview of how a battery becomes discharged, see page 46.)

If the charge indicator light comes on and stays on when you try to start up your car, then you probably have a discharged battery. Another way to tell if the battery is discharged is to look at the indicator eye on top of the battery. (Not all batteries have an indicator eye.) If the eye is black, the battery is discharged or dead.

Pop open the hood and put on some gloves. Examine the battery cable ends and the battery posts. Are they covered with a crusty white acid buildup? If so, clean them with a solution of baking soda and water, following the instructions on page 50. Check the fittings that secure the battery cables to the battery posts. Wiggle the battery cables. If the cable fittings seem loose, get out a wrench and tighten them. Check the amount of electrolyte in each of the battery cells, following the instructions on page 48 and top off with distilled water, if necessary.

If cleaning and topping off the battery won't get your car started, try jump-starting the battery. See page 208 for instructions. (If you can't clean and top off the battery right away, go ahead and try jump-starting, but be sure to get back to this battery maintenance task as soon as possible.)

Step 2: Check the Air Filter

If the battery seems fine — meaning that it is not caked with acid buildup, the cables are not loose, the electrolyte levels are fine, and jump-starting doesn't help — take a look at the air filter (see page 40 for details). If the filter needs to be replaced, it's a simple matter to install a new one. (And if you've followed the advice earlier in this chapter, you'll have a new air filter in the tool kit in the trunk of your car.)

Step 3: Check the Distributor Cap

If changing the air filter doesn't get your car to start up, move on to the distributor cap. Not all cars have distributor caps. If yours does, remove it and examine it carefully, following the instructions on page 206.

Step 4: Add Fuel Additive

Before you have the car towed to your mechanic's garage, ask yourself whether you recently filled up the gas tank. If the answer is yes, you may have a tank full of bad gas. Pour a small bottle of fuel additive into the gas tank, following the instructions on the product label. The additive will help clean impurities from the gas. If this little trick gets your car started, drive and drive until you have burned up some fuel. Then fill up again — at a different gas station, of course.

Step 5: Call for a Tow Truck

If you've made it from step 1 through step 4 and your car still won't start, have it towed to your mechanic's garage. She'll need to take a more in-depth look at the engine to determine and resolve the problem.

Checking the Distributor Cap

It's fairly easy to pick out the distributor cap under the hood. Not every car has a distributor cap, but if yours does, it will be a Medusa-like, blue or black cylinder with sturdy black wires extending up from it. (Turn to page 55 for more detail.) It's usually located right next to the engine block.

Make sure ignition is turned to "off" before you get started on this task.

TOOLS & SUPPLIES

- Flathead or Phillips head screwdriver, depending on the type of screw that secures your distributor cap in place
- Clean rag

1 **Remove the distributor cap.** Use a screwdriver to loosen or snap open the screws or clips that secure the distributor cap in place. Then wiggle the distributor cap loose.

2 **Examine the cap.** If the cap is damp on the inside, wipe it down with a clean rag. If the cap is cracked, you'll need to replace it. You can buy a new distributor cap and install it yourself, but you'll need to know the particulars of your car — make, model, year, number of cylinders. If you would prefer to have your mechanic do the job, book an appointment with her.

3 **Replace the cap.** Install the cap (new or old) on the distributor. Tighten the screws or clips that hold it in place.

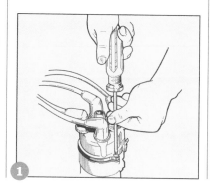

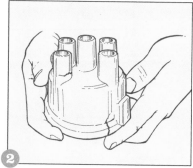

Jump-Starting a Battery

Before hooking up the jumper cables (also called booster cables) between two cars, take a minute to decide if the cars' batteries are compatible.

Some newer vehicles have computerized systems that can initiate a destructive electronic surge when jumper cables are hooked up to or removed from their batteries. Manufacturers of these and a few other types of vehicles recommend against jump-starting these batteries or using them to jump-start a battery in another car. Consult the owner's manuals for both cars; any NO JUMP-STARTING or NO BOOSTING warnings will be prominently displayed.

Make sure the batteries are the same type. Only a 12-volt battery should be used to jump-start a 12-volt battery. Similarly, only a 6-volt battery should be used to jump-start a 6-volt battery.

A vehicle that uses diesel fuel should never jump-start nor be jump-started by a vehicle that is not diesel-powered. Why? A battery in a diesel vehicle holds more electrical power than batteries in most conventional automobiles.

Take a look at the discharged battery. If you can open the vent caps, look inside to make sure that the electrolyte isn't frozen. (If one wall of the battery has a clear window, you can examine the electrolyte without opening the vent caps.) If the electrolyte in your discharged battery is frozen, a sudden flow of electrical current could cause the battery to explode. The only way to unfreeze a frozen battery is to bring it to a heated garage and let it thaw out.

Also check to make sure that the discharged battery has adequate levels of electrolyte (see page 48 for instructions). A battery that is low on electrolyte often exudes gases through its vent caps. These gases could explode if booster cables are hooked to its posts.

If the electrolyte is frozen or running low, don't jump-start. Call for a tow truck instead.

Examine the booster cables. Ideally, you should have 16-gauge cables that are at least 16 feet (5 m) long. Check the cables to make sure that no wiring is exposed; touching the wiring could give you an electrical shock once the cables are connected to the batteries.

Pre-Boosting Checklist

☐ Consult the owner's manuals for both cars to be sure that neither recommends against jump-starting.

☐ Make sure that both batteries are of the same voltage.

☐ Check the discharged battery to confirm that electrolyte levels are adequate and the electrolyte is not frozen.

☐ Examine the jumper cables; no wiring should be exposed.

In preparation for jump-starting a car, walk through the checklist at left. Then have the driver of the "live" vehicle move her car as close to the "dead" car as possible, but make sure the two vehicles do not touch.

TOOLS & SUPPLIES

• "Live" battery, either in another car or in a portable battery recharge kit

• Jumper or booster cables

1 Prepare the cars. Turn off all electrical accessories in both vehicles. In cars with an automatic transmission, shift into *P* (Park); in cars with manual transmissions, shift into *N* (Neutral). Set the parking brakes.

Turn the ignition key in both cars to the "off" position. (If the live battery has sufficient juice, the live vehicle doesn't need to be running to jump-start the discharged battery.)

2 Attach the positive cable. Hook the clamp of the positive (red) booster cable to the positive post on the discharged battery. Then hook the other end of

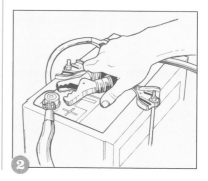

the positive booster cable to the positive post in the live battery.

③ Attach the negative cable. Hook the negative (black) booster cable to the negative post in the live battery. Then hook the other end of the negative booster cable to an unpainted metal part on the dead car. *Do not attach the negative cable to the discharged battery.* Place this clamp as far from the battery as possible.

④ Start up. After a couple of minutes, turn the ignition key in the dead car. If it starts up, leave it running and move onto the next step. If it doesn't start up, turn the ignition key back to the "off" position and leave the booster cables where they are. Try again in a few minutes.

⑤ Disconnect the negative cable. Remove the negative (black) booster cable from the formerly dead car. Then remove the negative cable from the live car.

⑥ Disconnect the positive cable. Remove the positive (red) booster cable from the live car.

Booster cable hookup

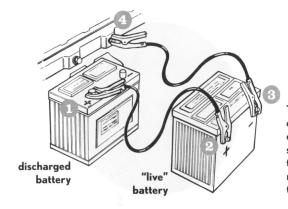

discharged battery

"live" battery

Then remove the positive cable from the formerly dead car.

⑦ Let the car run. Let the engine in the car that has been jump-started run for at least 15 minutes, either idling or as you drive. Running the engine recharges the battery.

To jump-start a battery, connect the booster cables in the order shown. When the battery is up and running, remove the cables in the reverse sequence.

When the Engine Overheats

An overheating engine is one of those curious affairs that are sometimes dangerous, sometimes innocuous, but always alarming. If your engine is *tending* to overheat, you can continue to drive, but you should bring the car to your mechanic immediately. Why? Because an engine that *does* overheat can experience serious — expensive — damage.

There are a lot of reasons why an engine might overheat, including:

- Low coolant level
- Frozen coolant
- Faulty cooling system component, such as the radiator cap, water pump, fan, or thermostat
- Leaking radiator core
- Leaking or burst radiator hoses
- Engine block leak
- Broken belt
- Stuck heater control valve
- Debris obstructing the radiator core
- Clogged heater core
- Clogged or kinked heater hose
- Clogged radiator
- Clogged radiator hose
- Insufficient engine oil

This is an extensive but not exhaustive list. Unfortunately, there's not much you can do to correct whatever malfunction is causing the engine to overheat. When the engine overheats, it probably needs a mechanic's attention. Your job is to make the right decision about what to do at the time that the engine becomes alarmingly hot. Here are three common scenarios.

Scenario #1. As you're driving, the temperature needle rises into the "hot" zone or the temperature indicator light comes on. Don't panic. If your car has air-conditioning, turn it off. Open the windows and turn on the heat to the highest setting — this will release heat from the engine into the passenger compartment. If you're in heavy stop-and-go traffic, shift the transmission into neutral and slowly rev the engine when you are temporarily stopped. Do not ride the brakes. Maintain some distance from the vehicle ahead of you to avoid having its hot exhaust fumes add heat to your car's already hot engine. You should see the temperature gauge needle drop to normal or the temperature indicator light shut off. Drive your car to the nearest mechanic.

Scenario #2. Scenario #1 has happened to you. You shut off the air-conditioning, opened the windows, and turned on the heat full blast. But the temperature gauge needle hasn't returned to the "normal" zone, or the temperature indicator light is still glowing. If this is the case, pick up from "Get off the road — now!" in Scenario #3, below.

Scenario #3. As you're driving, the temperature gauge needle rockets up to the "hot" zone or the temperature indicator light comes on, and steam starts billowing from under the hood. Get off the road — now! Turn off the ignition and get out of your car. Wait a few minutes to allow the engine to cool down and any steam to subside, then slowly open the hood and prop it open.

If you're uncomfortable approaching a hot engine, err on the side of caution. For the cost of a towing job, you can have your mechanic address the problem. If you have a cell phone, call for a tow truck. Otherwise, wait for help to arrive.

AUTOTALK

Here's an interesting point about human physiology: When exposed to searing heat, the muscles in the palms of your hands cause your hands to close, whereas muscles in the back of your hands pull away. Why is this important for you to know in an automotive emergency? If you must check hoses, tires, or other engine parts that tend to get hot, use the back of your hand, rather than the palm, to see whether they've cooled off enough for you to handle them.

(And consult What to Do If You're Stranded on page 219.)

If you're ready to do some investigating under the hood, there are a couple of do-it-yourself quick fixes that may help get your car back on the road long enough for you to drive it to the nearest auto repair shop. There's one important rule: *Allow the engine to cool completely before you start driving.* You should be able to touch the radiator with your bare hand.

Checking the Coolant

First check the level of coolant in the radiator. Wear gloves, and follow the instructions on page 70. If the radiator cap has a pressure-release device, open the lever using a flathead screwdriver, not your hand. Wait for the hissing from the cap to stop before completely removing the radiator cap.

The coolant should rise to just about 2 inches (5 cm) from the top of the radiator. It probably won't rise that high in your radiator — all that steam came from overflowing hot coolant splashing on hot engine parts. The radiator will probably be depleted of coolant.

Start up the engine and leave it running. Slowly pour water or premixed coolant into the radiator. Once the level of fluid rises to 2 inches (5 cm) below the top of the radiator, turn off the ignition. Let your car sit for a while, and then check the amount of coolant in the radiator.

OVERHEATING OVERVIEW

What You See	What You Do
The temperature gauge needle rises into the red zone or the temperature indicator light comes on	Turn off the air conditioning. Turn on the heat full blast. Drive your car immediately to a mechanic.
Turning off the air- conditioning and turning on the heat doesn't make the temperature gauge needle return to normal or the temperature indicator light shut off	Pull over. Call for a tow truck, or pop open the hood and check the coolant and the oil. Tow or drive the car immediately to a mechanic.
Steam billows out from under the hood	Pull over. Call for a tow truck, or wait for the steam to subside, then pop open the hood and check the coolant and the oil. Tow or drive your car immediately to a mechanic.

If necessary, continue adding water or coolant until there is sufficient fluid in the radiator. Make a note of how much water or coolant you've added, and relay this information to your mechanic as soon as you get your car to her garage.

It's important to add the water or coolant to the radiator and not the coolant recovery tank. Why? Coolant flows from the radiator, not the recovery tank. The recovery tank holds *excess* coolant, and right now you don't have an excess, you have a deficiency. Also, the hose extending from the recovery tank to the radiator, which enables the radiator to draw coolant from the recovery tank, may be plugged — in fact, if this hose is clogged, it may have contributed to the engine overheating.

Checking the Oil

The other component you can investigate as a possible cause of overheating is the oil. If the engine doesn't have sufficient lubrication, it will heat up. Check and, if necessary, top off the engine oil, following the instructions on page 82.

Getting On Your Way

Once the radiator seems to have an adequate amount of coolant and you've confirmed that there's enough engine oil in the oil pan, ease your car back onto the road. Keep the air-conditioning off and the heat on. Drive to the nearest auto repair shop or to your home, from where you can call your mechanic for a consultation.

If the engine overheats before you get to the auto repair shop, stop driving and call for a tow truck. Driving any further puts you at risk of severe engine damage.

Vapor Lock

When an engine gets super-hot — as might happen when you're driving uphill, driving at high altitudes, or stuck in stop-and-go traffic on a very hot day — gas in the fuel tank may actually begin to boil. Just as a pot of boiling water produces vaporous water, also known as steam, so a tank of boiling gasoline produces vaporous gasoline. If enough of the vapor passes into the fuel line, it blocks liquid fuel from reaching the fuel injectors. This is called vapor lock, and when it happens, the engine stops dead in its tracks. There is no rough idling, no gradual loss of power, no warning signs at all. Just one dead car.

If your car dies suddenly, with no growls, moans, or other symptoms, suspect vapor lock. Activate your hazard lights and get out of the car. If you can do so safely, push your car to the side of the road. Never work on your car while it is sitting in the middle of the road.

Once your car is safely off the road, pop open the hood. Now you must wait for the fuel to cool enough that the vapor returns to its liquid state and the blockage resolves itself. If you have the patience, you can sit it out and wait for the car to cool. You can also help it along by wrapping a wet rag around the fuel line.

Get a clean rag from the trunk and soak it in water (*never* gasoline or coolant). If you don't have a rag or water, reach into the tool kit in the trunk of your car and pull out a piece of aluminum foil. It serves the same function as a wet rag.

There are two places where you can access the fuel line to try to cool it down: under the car and under the hood. If you've done your homework, you've had your mechanic point out to you the fuel line in these two locations. If you can fit under the car, crawl underneath and wrap the wet rag around the fuel line, ideally between the fuel pump and fuel injection system. In some cars, the fuel pump is encased in the fuel tank (here's a great reason why it's so important to know the layout of your particular car). Be careful, because it will be hot under there — boiling gasoline, remember?

If you can't find the fuel line under the car, look for it under the hood and wrap the wet rag around it there.

If you have neither rag nor aluminum foil, you'll just have to be patient and let everything cool down. It takes a long time for a hot engine to cool down, and if the sun is blazing, you may even have to wait until nightfall, when the temperature drops. Be sure to keep yourself cool while you're waiting; wear a hat to keep the sun off your head and drink plenty of water.

If your car won't start even when the engine is cool the vapor lock may have caused the fuel filter to seize up. If this is the case, you'll have to have the car towed to your mechanic's garage.

Curing vapor lock under the hood

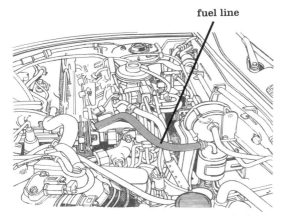

fuel line

The fuel line is one of many dusty black hoses at the back of the engine compartment. Have a mechanic point it out to you sometime so that you can find it in the event that your car suffers from vapor lock.

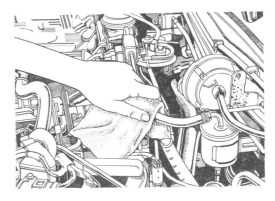

If you can't access the fuel line under the car, wrap the wet rag around the fuel line under the hood. Be careful, because the engine will be very hot, and keep your hands well away from belts and the fan.

What to Do After a Collision

As a responsible member of the driving public, you should take an active role if you're ever involved in a collision. Many drivers don't know what to do after a collision, and this causes them to panic. You, on the other hand, will be well informed and so are more likely to keep a clear head.

Fender Benders

If the collision caused only minor damage to either or both vehicles, drive both cars to a safe spot off the road, well away from traffic. Determine if you, the other driver, or any passengers in the cars require medical attention. If necessary, call 911 to have a medical team dispatched. Otherwise, call the local police station. While waiting for the police to arrive, begin filling out the collision report from the appendix.

Do not speak with the other driver about who was responsible for the collision; tempers can flare, and you don't want to be liable for words spoken in the heat of the moment.

By law, you *must* call the police in the event of an automobile collision. Leaving the scene of an accident, even a very minor one, can leave you vulnerable to criminal charges. Also, you won't be able to process your insurance claim — to have dents and scratches on your car repaired or to pay for repairs on the other vehicle — without a police report in hand. So even if the damage seems minuscule, stay put until the police arrive.

There is one exception to the "Don't leave the scene of an accident" rule. There have been inci-

---

Minor Collision Checklist

1. Move cars to side of road.
2. Check for injuries. Give first aid, if necessary.
3. Call 911 or the local police.
4. Fill out the collision report form in appendix.
5. Wait for help.

dents in which drivers have initiated fender benders in order to attack women. So if someone hits your car from behind while you're traveling alone, and it's dark outside or you're on an isolated stretch of road, take precautions. Pull over to the side of the road, but leave the engine idling and stay inside your car. As the other driver approaches you, make a note of what he or she and the vehicle behind you look like. If you can make out the license plate number of the vehicle, jot it down. Roll down your window just a bit and ask the other driver to follow you to the nearest police station or to a well-lit, well-populated location. Be assertive in this request; you don't have to be rude, but you must be determined not to let the other driver persuade you to get out of your car.

This cautionary approach may sound impractical, but it's not — it's safe. So don't hesitate to be cautious, and don't worry about leaving the scene of an accident — just drive straight to a safe location where you can, with full confidence of your personal safety, get out of your car and examine the extent of damage caused by the collision.

Major Collisions

If you are involved in a major collision, the highest priority is the health and safety of all drivers and passengers. Immediately turn off the engines of all vehicles involved. If you have or someone on location has a cell phone, call 911. Then, once you've ascertained that you are not hurt, check the passengers in your car and the occupants of the other vehicle. Give first aid when necessary. All those who can be safely moved — who are not trapped or suffering from neck or back

Major Collision Checklist

1. Turn off all car engines.

2. Call 911.

3. Check for injuries. Give first aid, if necessary.

4. Move all people who can be moved safely to the side of the road.

5. Wait for help.

injuries — should be moved to the side of the road, well away from traffic. Move vehicles only if they are obstructing traffic; otherwise, leave everything as is. Set out reflectors or flares (except if there is spilled fuel, which could ignite the flares) to warn oncoming motorists.

If no one involved in the accident has a cell phone (meaning that you are unable to call 911), someone must go for help. If possible, send a team of two people to find the nearest house or flag down a passing car. Those people who remain at the collision site should do their best to stay calm and warm until help arrives.

If You Hit an Unoccupied Vehicle

If you have a minor collision with an unoccupied vehicle and your car seems fine, it's okay to leave the scene, provided that you notify the owner of the other vehicle. Look in the appendix for the Collision Report — Unoccupied Vehicle. Fill it out completely and leave the bottom portion on the front windshield of the damaged vehicle.

The materials that body frames and fenders are made of these days are versatile but also expensive. Sometimes even just a small dent necessitates replacement of an entire frame unit. If you're unsure about the extent of repair that will be necessary for your car or the vehicle that you've damaged, call your insurance company for advice.

Unoccupied Vehicle Collision Checklist

1. Fill out the placard on page 254.

2. Leave the placard under the wiper blade on the front windshield of the damaged vehicle.

3. Write down the particulars of the incident, including all the information on the placard, for your own reference.

4. If you're in doubt about the extent of repair that is necessary for either your car or the unoccupied vehicle, call your insurance company for advice.

What to Do When You're Stranded

It sure is lonely on the side of the road. You stand there watching traffic sweep past or cows grazing in their pasture. You feel the cold wind whip through your jacket or the hot, humid air press down upon you. Probably it's raining. Soon you begin to wonder if you'll *ever* get to your destination. Your temper rises as you realize that your cell phone, which you purchased just for emergencies like this one, doesn't have reception at this particular spot. You hope that a traffic patrol officer will spot you soon. You wonder, with just a slight nod of recognition to your growing sense of paranoia, whether some lunatic will stop and harass you first.

When you're stranded, it's important to practice patience. Mistakes most often happen because someone was in a hurry to get going again. If you proceed calmly, confidently, and carefully, following the five-step process that follows, you'll be "unstranded" and on your way soon enough.

Step 1: Get Off the Road

If something is seriously wrong with your car, immediately switch on the hazard flashers. Safely make your way to the shoulder of the road. Pull as far away from the path of traffic as possible.

If your car has lost power in the middle of a busy road and you cannot move it, don't try to push it. Set the emergency brake, engage the hazard flashers, and prop open the hood.

Step 2: Put Out Warning Signals

If you're on the shoulder of the road, keep the hazard flashers on. Prop open the hood. Set out warning flares or reflective triangles; place one about ten car-lengths away from your car and place the other reflectors or flares between it and your car. Tie a white or brightly colored cloth to the radio antenna or the handle of the door that faces the road.

If your car is stuck in the middle of the road in busy traffic, the hazard flashers will have to suffice for warning. If there's a break in traffic or traffic is light, set out flares or reflective triangles well behind your car.

Step 3: Call for Help

If you have a cell phone or are near a pay phone, use it. If you're in familiar territory, call a local garage. If you don't have the number, call directory assistance (411 or your area code plus 555-1212). With a cell phone you can also dial 611 (or *611) to get in touch with a local cellular carrier customer service representative. If none of these options works, dial 911.

If you don't have a cell phone and a pay phone is not readily available, you'll have to wait for or go get help.

Step 4: Get Settled or Go for Help

How far away is the last town or service station you passed? If it's easily within walking distance, it may be worth your while to walk back. Before you head out, make sure you are dressed appropriately for the weather, and bring water with you. Also, turn to page 255 in the appendix and fill out the placard I'VE LEFT THE CAR ON FOOT TO FIND HELP. Place the placard on the dashboard of your car, so that it can be read from the outside. Leave a window open a crack and lock the doors before you go.

If someone other than a law enforcement officer stops to offer assistance, ask the driver to call for help; if the driver doesn't have a cell phone, perhaps he or she would be kind enough to stop at the next service station or rest area to make the call.

If the other driver offers you a lift, decline politely. Law enforcement agencies very strongly discourage women from hitching rides with strangers, and for good reason. Never get inside a vehicle with a stranger.

However, if, as a last, desperate, there's-no-other-solution resort, you've decided to ignore this very sound advice and hitch a ride with a stranger, at least take this precaution: Turn to page 256 in the appendix, tear out the placard I'VE HITCHED A RIDE IN ANOTHER CAR, and fill it out. If the other driver is not willing to show you his or her driver's license, absolutely do not get in the other vehicle. If the driver is accommodating and gives you all the information you need, leave the placard on the dashboard of your car, so that it can be read from the outside the car. Leave a window open a crack and lock the doors of your disabled car before you go.

If you're not near a town or service station — or if you don't know where you are — your safest option is to stay with the car. Most highways are regularly patrolled by law enforcement officers, who will stop to assist stranded travelers. The police may not give you a ride to the garage, but they will call for help, and they should stay with you until help arrives.

If your car is on the side of the road, take what you need from the trunk and get comfortable in the front seat, on the side away from traffic. (For example, if you're pulled over on the right side of the road, you'd sit in the passenger's seat.) Lock all the doors and roll up all the windows; leave one open just enough to allow some fresh air to flow inside. Place a HELP sign (see page 257) in the back window. Get comfortable, remain calm, and rest assured that help will come.

If your car is not on the side of the road or is not well removed from traffic, get what you need from the trunk — a blanket, extra clothing, food, water, and so on — and walk to the shoulder of the road. Find a safe spot where you have good visibility to the road and settle in.

Step 5: Get a Lift

When a tow truck finally arrives at the site where your car is disabled, remain calm and cooperative. Verify that the driver offering assistance is from the garage that you contacted. Ride with the tow truck driver to the garage.

Once you're at the garage, have the mechanic perform an evaluation and then give you an estimate for the repair work that is required. Ask her to detail the repairs in writing before you agree to have the work performed. If need be, take this book in hand and verify what you've been told with what's in these pages. You want to show the mechanic that you are an informed automobile owner who may not necessarily know how to change a water pump, for example, but you do know what one is and what is involved in replacing it.

When You're *Really* Stranded

While it's not likely that you'll ever find yourself stranded on a seldom-traveled mountain pass or a lonely stretch of desert, it's still wise to be prepared for even worst-case scenarios. If you've followed the advice given earlier and prepared an emergency kit with water, food, and appropriate clothing, you should be equipped to handle any emergency situation.

The best thing to do when you're *really* stranded is to stay put — someone at home will realize that you've been gone too long or someone who's expecting you at the other end will realize that you're overdue. For a search team, it's infinitely easier to find a disabled car than to find a lone human body wandering through nature. And your car will offer warmth at night.

While you're waiting for help to arrive, you should make your car as visible as possible. Mark a big X on the roof with reflective tape or lipstick. Place a HELP or POLICE sign in the front or back window. Tie white or brightly colored rags to nearby trees and bushes. Start a small fire and toss in engine oil or bits of rubber from your car to create thick, dark smoke. (Of course, first clear the area of all weeds and brush, secure the fire with rocks, have water to douse the fire on hand, and monitor the fire carefully — the next worst thing to being stranded in the middle of nowhere is being stranded in the middle of a forest fire!)

Surviving Extreme Cold

If you're stranded in a blizzard, it's safer to stay inside your car than to walk to get help. Your most important concern is staying warm. Your car will offer some protection from the elements. You can add to the insulating effect by padding the outside of your car, including the underside but excluding the tailpipe, with snow. Be absolutely sure that snow doesn't obstruct your tailpipe; if the exhaust system is blocked, carbon monoxide fumes will be forced into your car when the engine is running. Every hour, walk around to the back of your car to make sure the tailpipe is clear of snow.

Insulate the inside of the windows and any exposed metal parts with carpets, newspaper, rubber floor mats — whatever you have available. Set a candle in an empty metal cup and place it on the dashboard. (A lit candle inside your car offers a surprising amount of heat.) Bundle yourself up in the front seat; don't sit on the floor, as cold tends to seep in from the bottom of the car. To conserve your body heat, always wear a hat. If your car still has power, run the engine for ten minutes every hour to keep the battery charged and to generate heat.

Most important, stay awake. When you sleep, your body temperature drops. If it's already freezing in the car, you'll freeze to death while you sleep. To stay awake, keep yourself occupied. Write notes, such as the time you stopped, the date, and what and when you've eaten. Constantly change your position. Sing to your heart's content. Write that long overdue novel!

Surviving Extreme Heat

If you're stranded far from civilization in blazing heat and dry conditions, obviously it's important to stay cool and hydrated. However, achieving this when your only shelter is your car can be difficult.

If there are any trees or brush nearby, seek shelter in whatever shade they provide. Only you, your car, and a long stretch of road? Sit next to your car, in its shadow. If the car is on pavement, push it over to the dirt or grass at the side of the road, so that you're not absorbing radiant heat from the blacktop.

You can also use extra clothing and blankets from your emergency kit to create a shaded area. Drape them over an open car door and the top of the car as if you were making a tent.

Keeping your head covered will also help you stay cool. If you're not wearing a hat, drape extra clothing over the top of your head.

Your emergency kit should also contain food and water. Use both sparingly. Never drink any fluids from under the hood — they're poisonous.

If you decide that the only way you're going to get out of this mess is to walk to civilization, take all the supplies with you that you can carry and fill out the placard on page 255 and leave it in your car before you go. Above all, don't decide that a shortcut through the bush will save you time. Stay on the main road.

THE REAL LOWDOWN ON DETAILING

L ooking good out on the road is important to some enthusiastic drivers, but other motorists think it's ridiculous to spend all that time and money just to have a spotless, gleaming car. Regardless of your persuasion, proper detailing — attending to the durability and appearance of your car's interior and exterior — is important. Why? Not only will a car that is properly cared for last longer, but it will also have better resale value than a car that is not properly cared for. Clean seats, a sparkling dashboard, crystal-clear windows, a shiny exterior, glossy black tires, and no scratches, rust, or dents — all this and more can be yours for investing in just a few precautionary steps, some periodic minor repairs, and a Saturday morning every once in a while. When it does come time to sell your car, the long-term benefits of proper detailing will display themselves in your pocketbook.

Cleaning Out Your Car

Keeping the interior of your car clean is a lot like plain old housekeeping. Practice neatness. Dust regularly. Vacuum. If someone spills something on the "furniture" — a car seat or the floor — wipe it up and, if necessary, treat it with a stain remover. The total process can be broken down into six easy steps:

1. Pick up.
2. Vaccuum.
3. Clean the seats and floor.
4. Apply stain repellent.
5. Clean vinyl surfaces.
6. Wash the windows.

This six-step plan is simple but all-inclusive. Undertaken faithfully every couple of weeks or months, these commonsense maintenance practices will keep your car looking, feeling, and smelling like new for years to come.

Pick 'em Up

Is your backseat laden with empty coffee cups, pencils, papers, hamburger wrappers, loose change, and everything else you've brought into your car over the past couple of weeks? It looks — well, let's face it — sloppy. Your lifestyle habits are not at issue here, though. What is a concern is your safety. If you have to stop suddenly or are involved in a collision, a loose object inside your car becomes a deadly weapon. It's simple "G-force" physics. For example, a few years ago a local paper ran a story about a woman who suffered head injuries in a low-speed collision because a box of tissues hit her in the head.

For safety's sake, keep the front and back seats, dashboard, and the back window ledge free of loose objects.

- Keep loose change sealed in a small baggie or change purse in the glove compartment.
- If you travel with children, secure toys in a closed plastic bin. Remove only one or two toys at a time. The toys themselves should not have sharp edges or metal parts. Teach children to take their garbage with them when they get out of the car.

- Line a small cardboard box with a plastic bag and keep it in your car as a garbage receptacle. (The box will also be useful in the event that one of your passengers develops a case of motion sickness.)
- Once a week, unclutter your car. Empty the garbage box and find a different home for the papers, clothing, bags, wrappers, and other loose items that have snuck into the car.

Vacuum

To keep the seats and floor clean and free of odors, vacuum the inside of your car at least once a month. Remove the rubber floor mats and vacuum beneath them. Use the slim, angled head of the vacuum cleaner to suck crumbs and dirt from the crack where the seat backs and seat cushions meet, as well as all around the safety belt attachments. And while you're at it, vacuum the trunk, too.

If you don't have a vacuum cleaner that you can use outside, drive your car to a car wash. Most have high-powered vacuums that you can use for the cost of the loose change you'll have found inside your car when you picked up.

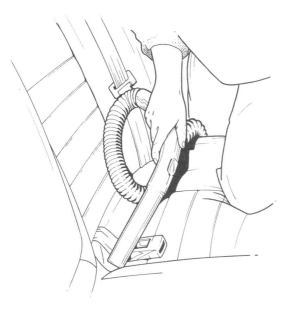

Vacuum carefully around seat belt buckles, even using the angled head to suck crumbs out from inside each buckle. Then use a clean cloth to wipe down the outside of each buckle. Careful maintenance will keep the buckles functioning safely for the lifetime of your vehicle.

AUTOTALK

If you're on the road and you spill something that you think is going to leave a stain in the car, treat the stain just as you would if it were on the sofa in your living room: Use a clean cloth to mop it up as best you can, then apply a stain remover. If you don't have a commercial stain remover readily available, sop the stain with soda water. In most cases, it'll be just as effective as a commercial stain remover. For emergencies — like when your child finally learns to open the lid on her "childproof" cup, which at the moment happens to be filled with chocolate milk — keep a small bottle of soda water in the tool kit you have stowed in the trunk of your car.

Clean the Seats and Floor

After you vacuum, wipe clean the seats. Most cars have cloth seats; some luxury vehicles and SUVs are fitted with leather seats. Purchase a commercial cleaning product suitable for the fabric in your car. You don't need a special "automotive" cleaning product for this task; any commercial fabric cleaner or leather conditioner will do. Follow the instructions on the product label.

Check the carpet for stains. Treat any stain, no matter how small or large, with a commercial carpet stain–removing product.

Apply Stain Repellent

If you have cloth seats and a carpeted floor, once you've vacuumed and cleaned them apply a stain repellent such as ScotchGuard. This will protect the seats and floor from acquiring stains in the future.

Be sure that you've scrubbed away any visible stains before spraying on the stain repellent. If you apply repellent over a stain, that stain becomes permanently embedded in the fabric.

Clean Vinyl Surfaces

Use a commercial vinyl cleaner/protectant to dust and shine the dashboard, armrests, door trim, and other vinyl surfaces in your car. Follow the instructions on the product label. The cleaner/protectant leaves vinyl looking like new, and it also protects these areas against sunlight and excessive heat.

AUTOTALK

To prevent vinyl from fading or cracking, park your car away from direct sunlight whenever possible. If you must park your car in the sun, keep a window open a crack to allow heat to escape.

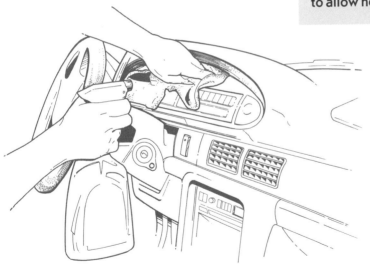

In addition to making the dashboard sparkle, vinyl cleaner protects the vinyl surface from heat and sunlight and minimizes the dust that gets blown around inside the car when you turn on the heat or air-conditioning.

Wash the Windows

Over time, a thin film of grime builds up on the inside of windows. (If you smoke in your car, this happens much faster.) This gray coating can interfere with your ability to see the road, other motorists, and pedestrians.

Car windows can be washed much like house windows. Use a solution of vinegar and water or a commercial glass cleaner. If your rear window defroster is made up of thin metal wires running across the window, be gentle. Those wires are set on the inside of the window, and you don't want to damage them. Use gentle horizontal strokes to clean the window, moving in the same direction as the wires, not against them.

Cleaning the inside of the windows gives you improved visibility, particularly when the sun is glaring off the windshield or when the windows are fogged up.

Washing and Waxing

Forget the aesthetics. To keep your car from rusting out beneath you, you must keep the exterior clean. Washing a car regularly keeps road salt, mud, and other grime from lodging in the nooks and crannies of your car (places where rust usually gets a first foothold). And having a sparkling clean car makes you more visible on the road, especially in inclement weather.

While wax doesn't add to your car's visibility on the road, it certainly does help prevent rust. Think down the road to the time when you're going to sell your car. Who's going to want to buy a car that looks like a rusty bucket? Drivers who live in the North, where salt is used to keep the roads clear during winter, know firsthand that salt and car bodies don't mix. Mud can also be an instigator for rust. Even if you live in automobiling paradise, where the weather is always temperate, your car will benefit from regular washing and periodic waxing.

Clean is safe, clean is cool, and clean is definitely a roadworthy defense against sour looks from other drivers who are offended by the occasional rust and dirt that most of us must live with. So keep it clean! Here's how.

Soap and Suds

There are plenty of automated car washes and coin-operated self-service car washes; you've probably seen one in your neighborhood. Washing your car in the driveway of your home does have advantages, however. For one, you can take a time out to sip a cold glass of iced tea as you proudly examine your car-washing accomplishments. Follow these simple guidelines and you'll end up with a well-washed piece of automotive machinery:

- Wash your car only when its body is cool.
- Keep your car out of direct sunlight when you are washing, drying, or waxing it.
- Wash the wheels first, and then the car body from the top to the bottom.
- Use cold water and a commercial car-washing detergent, not dish detergent or laundry soap (they're too harsh for the paint and finish on your car).

The tires are usually the dirtiest part of your car, so it's wise to start with them. Spray-wash all four tires and then the underside of your car, including the wheel wells, to remove gravel, mud, sand, and other grime. Using a scrub brush, thoroughly clean the tires and rims. This is not the time to skimp on soap and suds.

When you're ready to wash the body of the car, read and follow the instructions on the label of the car-washing detergent. Use a steady flow of water from the garden hose to wash and rinse the car, working from top to bottom. A garden hose with a spray nozzle is much more effective than a bucket of water for cleaning your car. If you use a bucket, the water gets dirty quickly, and soon you

find yourself washing and rinsing with dirty water — not the ideal way to get the car clean.

Towel-dry all areas with a soft cloth. Remember to dry the hard-to-get-at places like around the chrome and inside the wheel wells.

CAUTION

When you are washing your car, never open the hood and spray-wash the engine. Water coming in contact with the electrical wiring will cause a short circuit, and if moisture accumulates in the air filter, your car will stall or even not start at all.

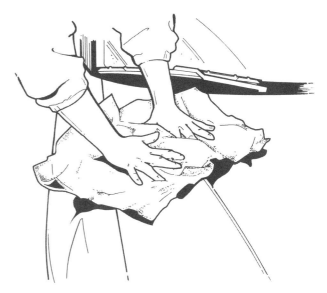

To avoid streaks, follow the contours of the car with the drying cloth, rather than rubbing in a circulation motion.

Dressed-Up Tires

After all the tires on your car have dried, apply a silicone lubricant to the tire walls (*not* the tread). This lubricant helps preserve the tires, and it gives them that glossy black appearance they haven't had since the day you first took them on the road. Silicone lubricants are available at auto parts stores. Follow the instructions on the product label.

If your tires have whitewalls — white trim on the sidewall — you can obtain a whitewall cleaner designed to make the white whiter.

Silicone lubricant can interfere with the gripping action of tire treads, so use it to polish only the sides of the tires.

Removing Sticky Stuff

Removing sticky stuff from the body of your car can be a real time-consuming pain. And if you end up scratching the paint in the process — argh! Here are a few tricks of the trade to make the job simpler.

Bird droppings and tree sap. Drape a wet cloth over the area to soften it up. After about 15 minutes, try wiping up the mess with the cloth. (*Up* is the operative word — you don't want to push the droppings or sap across more of the car body than it already occupies.) You may have to do this a few times before the spot is completely cleaned up.

Bumper stickers. Turn a blow-dryer to the high heat setting. Direct the flow of hot air over one end of the bumper sticker. As the paper heats up, the adhesive will liquefy, allowing you to peel the paper from the car. Slowly work your way from one end of the sticker to the other. If any of the adhesive is left on the car after you've removed all the paper, rubbing over it with a small amount of rubbing alcohol should clean it up.

Decals. To remove a decal from a window in your car, use a blow-dryer as directed above.

There will probably be glue left on the window once the decal is removed. Use a razor blade to scrape it away. Be careful and methodical; you don't want to scratch the window or, more important, cut yourself.

Shampooing the Engine

A clean engine performs better than a dirty engine. The first step in cleaning the engine involves degreasing (removing dirt and grease from) all the engine components. There are degreasing products available to consumers, but using them is a sticky, challenging job. You might consider, instead, taking your car to a professional car care center. For a not unreasonable price, the professional staff at the center will use the proper techniques to prerinse, degrease, and then apply a special dressing compound to the engine. Car-washing professionals call this premium treatment "shampooing the engine."

Even if you don't undertake degreasing the engine yourself, there are a few things you can do at home as a measure of good maintenance. Every month, use a clean, dry rag to wipe away grease, dirt, and other grime from the upper and lower radiator hoses, the air cleaner, the tops of the windshield washer fluid and coolant reservoirs, underneath the hood, and the top of the battery. Wipe clean the battery last, so that you don't transfer acid buildup onto other components under the hood.

Waxing

Research shows that waxing helps keep your car from getting small rust spots (which lead to larger rust spots), especially in the nooks and crannies at the fender and wheel wells. But waxing a car has an abysmal reputation as a time-consuming, patience-challenging task. You have the option of having your car waxed by a professional detailer, but it's actually not as hard to do it yourself as you might think. An afternoon of dry weather, some basic supplies, a stretch of patience, and — voilà! A finished product you're sure to be proud of.

If you decide to wax the car yourself, one of your toughest tasks will be picking out the wax. There are shelves full of them at most auto parts stores. If you have a newer car, its body paint is most likely finished with a clear coat; that is, the top coat of paint has no color in it. The clear coat is designed to protect the finish on your car. When you shop for a wax, look for one that is labeled CLEAR COAT SAFE.

Car wax generally comes in three types: liquid, soft, and hard. Liquid waxes tend to be the easiest to use. You apply the wax, let it dry, then wipe it off with a soft cloth and buff the car with another soft cloth. The wax dries quickly and is difficult to remove if it overdries, so you must work from one small area on your car to another. Above all else, be sure that your car is not parked in the sun while you're waxing it. Sunlight causes spotting in a new coat of wax, which will make the car look worse than when you got started.

Polishing

Detailing is in the details. After you've washed and waxed your car, take a few extra minutes to polish the chrome and metal surfaces of your car using an automotive chrome polish, following the instructions on the product label. Depending on the make and model of your car, chrome and metal can be found on everything from headlight casings to door handles to tire rims. Chrome polish can damage paint, so proceed carefully and keep the product off the body of your car.

After polishing, further protect these areas by applying a wax designed for chrome and metal surfaces. (Both chrome polish and chrome wax are available at auto parts stores.)

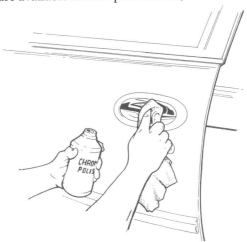

Polishing the small bits of chrome on your car, like the door handles, can do as much as washing and waxing to keep your car looking like new.

Rust, Scratches, and Dents

A couple of scratches, a rust spot, or a minor dent can make your car look aesthetically unpleasing. Repairing minor scratches and dents shouldn't be an expensive endeavor, whether you do the job yourself or bring the car to a body shop. (A body shop is the automotive equivalent of a plastic surgeon. While your mechanic handles all of your car's mechanical problems, staff at a body shop are trained to deal with cosmetic repairs, from minor scratches and dents to crumpled fenders and smashed windshields.)

But it's easy to botch a do-it-yourself bodywork job. Take a rust spot, for example. Unless you have a trained eye, what you think is just a small rust spot may actually be a small rust spot *and* a small hole. When you sand down the rust, you find the hole. Now you have to go back to the auto parts store to buy filler. When you get home, you have a lot of intensive hands-on work to do to fill in the hole, smooth down the spot, and paint over it. When all is said and done, you find that the touch-up paint that was supposed to match the color of your car doesn't. Perhaps it was the wrong paint. Perhaps the color of the paint on your car has faded. Who knows? But now you've thrown your money and your time into a futile effort that a professional could have undertaken successfully for the price of the massage you're going to need to soothe your frustration.

Why not, instead, talk with the staff at a body shop to get their opinion and an estimate on the bodywork that needs to be done? It certainly won't empty your wallet to have a professional repair the types of minor dents and dings that you would be able to tackle yourself. And the cost of a professional job might well be worth it if you can avoid the possibility of causing further cosmetic damage to your car.

Finding a Good Body Shop

Finding a reputable body shop requires some investigation. If you have a good relationship with your mechanic, ask her for a recommendation. And, as with any new service, check out the shop itself. Is the customer service area presentable? Do employees seem knowledgeable and courteous? Will they give you a detailed cost estimate?

When a body shop staff member gives you an estimate of how much it will cost to repair your car, review it carefully. If there is anything you don't understand or that seems to be missing, ask questions. In other words, be sure that your expectations match those of the body shop staff.

You might also inquire whether the shop keeps all the work in-house (some body shops send portions of their work to other venues) and whether the shop guarantees its work (quality body shops guarantee their work for as long as you own your car).

Once the staff have finished with the repair, closely inspect the work. Be sure you are pleased with the work and comfortable with the final bill before leaving the shop. If the work isn't what you expected or the bill seems too high, ask the staff to explain why. If their explanation doesn't satisfy you, ask to see the manager. Don't underestimate your role as a consumer. Being nasty isn't the goal — communication and coming to a resolution is. If the work is excellent and the estimate was right on, thank everyone for their help. Let the manager know that you'll be bringing your car back whenever it needs bodywork and that you'll recommend the shop to your family and friends.

AUTOTALK

A dent on your car may be a repair you can do yourself. This may sound silly, but in some cases you can use a toilet plunger to suction out a small dent. (Moisten the edge of the rubber cup so that it sticks to the car body.) You may have to try this a few times to get the right grip pressure to pull the indented section back into place. You can also use a hammer to lightly tap out the extended end of the dent from inside the car body. Cover the hammer with a rag so you don't make a new dent while trying to fix the existing dent.

APPENDIX

Vehicle Specifications Record

Cut out this form and attach a color photograph of your car that shows its license plate number. Keep it in a safe place in your home.

Vehicle Specifications Record

Year: _____   Make: _____

Model: _____   Color: _____

Engine size: _____   Cylinders: _____

Torque (lb./ft.): _____   Horsepower: _____

License plate number: _____

Air-conditioning: ☐ Yes   ☐ No

Vehicle Identification Number (VIN): _____

Ignition key number: _____   Air filter number: _____

Oil filter number: _____   Engine oil type: _____

Gasoline type: _____   Tire size: _____

Tire pressure: _____

Insurance company: _____

   Telephone number: _____

      Policy number: _____

Weekly Maintenance Checks

fluid levels

FLUID	PROBLEMS NOTICED If you discover any problems in your check or have to top off the fluid, note here. Include the date.	DATE SERVICED If your mechanic drains the fluid and replaces it with new fluid, note the service in this column. Include the date.
Engine oil		
Automatic transmission fluid or clutch fluid		
Brake fluid		
Power steering fluid		
Coolant		
Windshield washer fluid		

tires

TIRE LOCATION	AIR PRESSURE If you have to add more air to a tire, note it here. Include the date.	TREAD WEAR Note the tread wear pattern (see pages 110–111).
Front driver's side		
Front passenger's side		
Rear driver's side		
Rear passenger's side		
Spare tire		

Weekly Maintenance Checks continued on page 242

Weekly Maintenance Checks (continued)

exterior bulbs

BULB	PROBLEMS NOTICED If you discover any problems in your check, note them here. Include the date.	DATE CHANGED Note the date upon which you or your mechanic replaced the bulb.
Headlights (low beam)		
Headlights (high beam)		
Front left turn signal		
Front right turn signal		
Rear left turn signal		
Rear right turn signal		
Rear brake lights		
Hazard flashers		

Monthly Maintenance Checks

Component	Problems Noticed If you discover any problems in your check, note them here. Include the date.	Date Serviced If you or your mechanic serviced any of these components, note the service performed. Include the date.
Upper radiator hose		
Lower radiator hose		
Air filter		
Battery		
Shock absorbers		
Windshield wiper blades		
Horn		
Tire inflation valves and stems		

Vehicle Tune-Up

COMPONENT	SERVICE
three months	
Engine oil	Change oil and filter
six months	
Air-conditioning unit	Check for leaks and check refrigerant level
Air filter	Replace if dirty
Battery	Perform a battery load test
Body parts	Lubricate all moving parts (door locks and hinges, glove compartment hinge, visor hinge, trunk lock and hinge)
Brakes	Check pads and shoes and replace if worn
Coolant	Test strength and check for leaks
Exhaust system	Check all parts for wear and check for loose clamps and hangers
Fuel filter	Check condition and replace if necessary
Fuel-injection system	Conduct a computer systems check
Headlights	Adjust if aimed too high or too low
Hoses and belts	Check for cracks, fraying edges, and other worn spots; replace if necessary
Parking brake	Check cable tension and tighten if necessary

Component	Service
Pedals	Test gas, brake, and clutch pedals for tightness
Spark plugs	Check all spark plugs and their wires; replace if necessary
Suspension	Check shock absorbers or struts as well as other suspension components for wear; replace if necessary
Tires	Check alignment
Transmission	Check quality and quantity of fluid; check for leaks
Windshield wiper blades	Replace on both the front and rear windshields

two years

Component	Service
Automatic transmission (if you have one)	Replace filter and fluid inside the pan
Brake fluid	Flush and refill braking system
Fuel filter	Install new filter
Ignition system	Test electrical current; check for frayed wires
Cooling system	Flush and refill cooling system
Radiator hoses	Install new hoses and clamps
Spark plugs and spark plug wires	Replace all spark plugs and wires
Thermostat	Install new thermostat and gasket

Collision Report Form

YOUR VEHICLE

Insurance company: _____

    Insurance company's phone number: _____

    Your policy number: _____ Exp. date: _____

License plate number: _____

Driver's license number: _____ Exp. date: _____

Damage to your vehicle (where it is and the extent of damage):

_____

_____

_____

_____

_____

_____

_____

_____

_____

_____

_____

_____

OTHER VEHICLES

Obtain the following information from each of the other vehicles involved in the collision.

Name of driver: _____

Driver's home address: _____

A.M. phone: _____ P.M. phone: _____

Driver's license number: _____ Exp. date: _____

Make: _____ Model: _____ Year: _____ Color: _____

Vehicle license plate number: _____

Vehicle identification number: _____

Insurance company's name: _____

Insurance company's phone number: _____

Policy number: _____ Exp. date: _____

Damage to the other vehicle (where it is and the extent of damage):

_____

_____

_____

_____

Collision Report Form continued on page 248

Collision Report Form (continued)

DIAGRAM OF COLLISION SCENE *(be as specific as possible)*

EVENTS LEADING TO THE COLLISION *(be as specific as possible)*

Date of collision: _____ Time of collision: _____

Location of collision: _____

Weather conditions: _____

Road conditions: _____

Traffic congestion: _____

Nearby traffic signals or signs: _____

SPECIFICS ABOUT YOUR VEHICLE

Direction of your travel: _____

Skid marks: ☐ Yes   ☐ No   Estimated length of skid marks _____

Your speed: Accurate _____   Estimated _____

What were you doing when the collision occurred? (Write down that you were, for example, waiting at a stoplight, signaling for a turn, or driving in the right-hand lane.) _____

_____

Other remarks: _____

_____

_____

Collision Report Form continued on page 250

Collision Report Form (continued)

SPECIFICS ABOUT THE OTHER VEHICLES

Obtain the following information for each of the other vehicles involved in the collision.

Direction of vehicle's travel: _____

Skid marks: ☐ Yes ☐ No Estimated length of skid marks _____

Other vehicle's speed: Accurate _____ Estimated _____

What was the other vehicle doing when the collision occurred? (Write down that it was, for example, waiting at a stoplight, signaling for a turn, or driving in the right-hand lane.)_____

_____

_____

Other remarks:_____

_____

_____

_____

_____

Persons Involved in the Accident

For each of the occupants of your car, including yourself, as well as all occupants in the other vehicle(s) involved in the collision, obtain the following information. If any pedestrians were involved in the collision, include them in this listing.

Occupant	Contact Phone	Injuries?	Extent of Injury

Collision Report Form continued on page 252

Collision Report Form (continued)

YOUR STORY

In your own words, write down everything you can remember that led up to the collision, even if you think it is irrelevant.

_____

_____

_____

_____

_____

_____

_____

_____

_____

_____

_____

_____

_____

_____

POLICE OFFICERS

Names of responding officers: _____

Badge numbers: _____

Collision file number: _____

WITNESSES

Obtain the following information from any witnesses to the collision.

Witness	Daytime Phone	Nighttime Phone

Unoccupied Vehicle Collision Report Form

If you damage a vehicle that is unoccupied, fill in this report, cut off the bottom portion, and leave it under a windshield wiper on the front windshield of the damaged vehicle.

THE VEHICLE I HIT

Year:_____ Make:_____ Model:_____ Color:_____

Description of damage: _____

Preexisting dents, scrapes, and other damage on the vehicle:_____

_____

My apologies — I damaged your car! Please give me a call when you receive this notice.

Today's date: _____ Time: _____

My name: _____

My A.M. phone: _____ My P.M. phone:_____

The damage is as follows:_____

_____

_____

Leaving the Car on Foot to Find Help

If you are leaving your vehicle to walk, fill out this placard and place it faceup on the dashboard of your car. Lock the doors before you go.

I'VE LEFT THE CAR ON FOOT TO FIND HELP

Today's date: _____ Time I left: _____ ☐ A.M. ☐ P.M.

My name: _____

Name of contact person: _____

    Daytime phone: _____ Nighttime phone: _____

I am alone ☐ OR I am with _____ adults and _____ children

I or my companions have been injured: ☐ Yes   ☐ No

    The injuries are: _____

_____

My food supplies are: _____

My water supply is: _____

I am heading in this direction: _____

I will be leaving these signs on my path: _____

_____

Hitching a Ride

If you hitch a ride with another car, fill out this placard and place it face-up on the dashboard of your car. **Remember:** Never get into a vehicle if the driver will not give you the personal information you need to fill out the placard.

I'VE HITCHED A RIDE IN ANOTHER CAR

Today's date: _____ Time I left: _____ □ A.M. □ P.M.

My name: _____

Name of contact person: _____

   Daytime phone: _____ Nighttime phone: _____

I am alone □ OR I am with _____ adults and _____ children

I or my companions have been injured: □ Yes □ No

   The injuries are: _____

Name of the person who is giving me a ride: _____

   Address: _____

   Daytime phone: _____ Nighttime phone: _____

Driver's license number: _____ State of registration: _____

Vehicle license number: _____

Physical description of driver: _____

We are driving to: _____

INDEX

Italicized references indicate an illustration; bold references indicate a chart.